The

Amazonian Chronicles

The Amazonian Chronicles

BY JACQUES MEUNIER & A. M. SAVARIN
TRANSLATED BY CAROL CHRISTENSEN

Mercury House
San Francisco

© Éditions Phébus, Paris, 1991.
All rights reserved under International and Pan-American Copyright
Conventions. Originally published in French as
Le Chant du Silbaco: Chronique Amazonienne
English translation copyright © 1994 by Carol Christensen

Published in the United States by
Mercury House
San Francisco, California

United States Constitution, First Amendment: Congress shall make no law respecting an establishment of religion, or prohibiting the free exercise thereof; or abridging the freedom of speech, or of the press; or the right of the people peaceably to assemble, and to petition the Government for a redress of grievances.

Cover photo by Eleanor Hopewell of Ethnic Arts of Berkeley. The woman is of the Ashinancha tribe, living on the Ene River in Peru. Her photo is set against the fabric of a purse she wove and painted for her husband.

Mercury House and colophon are registered trademarks of
Mercury House, Incorporated

Printed on acid-free paper
Manufactured in the United States of America

Library of Congress Cataloging-in-Publication Data
Meunier, Jacques, 1941–
[Chant du Silbaco. English]
The Amazonian chronicles / Jacques Meunier, A. M. Savarin.
Translated by Carol Christensen.
p.   cm.
Translation of: Chant du Silbaco.
ISBN 1-56279-053-6 : $20.00
1. Indians of South America—Amazon River Region—Social life and customs.
2. Ethnology—Amazon River Region.   3. Man—Influence on nature—Amazon River Region.   4. Amazon River Region—Social life and customs.   5. Amazon River Region—Description and travel.
I. Savarin, A. M. (Anne-Marie)   II. Title.
F2519.1.A6M413   1994
981'.1—dc20   93-12724
CIP
5   4   3   2   1

TO FANNY

TABLE OF
CONTENTS

TRANSLATOR'S NOTE: "THE WORLD STARTS WITH A STORY"

THE VOICE OF A STORY-teller in the profound darkness of a forest night. At the end of *The Amazonian Chronicles,* the ethnologists are sitting among a group of Indians around a dying fire, listening to a pair of stories, tribal myths: two tales of severed heads. Each story relates past events that affect the present and future. One leaves the listener haunted by a threat—a severed head still wanders the forest, rolling through the underbrush near the most-used paths, desperate to attach itself to the unwary traveler; the storyteller asks, "Have you ever seen it?" In the other story, a severed head is transformed into the moon, tethered to the earth by a thread and linked to the endless cycles of women's pain, bleeding and birthing.

The listeners raise their eyes above the treetops to stare at the sky and see a new star blinking in the firmament. A satellite.

A fitting image for a world that stretches from preliterate society—from the Amazon Indians for whom the authors' journal, the web of notes in which they try to capture their subject, are meaningless marks on a page—to the world of modern physics that has read marks in the sky to create a new network of meaning, an international communication network that holds the uneasy promise of a global village and a postliterate society.

From this modern image of the earth viewed from space—this magical vision of the entire planet—Meunier and Savarin's book has grown. Their plea to preserve Amazonia and its Indians is an ecological argument: "Defenders of modernization say, 'The end of a tribe is not the end of the world.' Ethnology never claimed that it was! But ethnology does see in it the end of a world and the loss of a human potential: the diminishment of the human space." With the destruction of the primitive world, "The number of ways of being human grows smaller. Consciousness become standardized. Our range of choices is reduced.... We watch powerless as the drama of our own impoverishment is enacted."[1]

The loss they fear most is the loss of the imaginative or dream world, the Indians' "ability to discover the mythic dimension in every event."[2] This is the art Meunier and Savarin would bring to anthropology. It is this dual vision, the ability to "travel in the world of myths and ideas," that allows them to create a book that joins "theory and practice," science and passion, poetry and politics.

Meunier and Savarin are not romantics of adventure or tourists of exoticism. Their guidebooks include chronicles, journals, visionary travelogues. Describing the conquest of the Amazon from the arrival of Spanish and Portuguese soldiers and missionaries to subsequent waves of gold seekers, rubber barons, ranchers, and land speculators, they portray the social and economic realities threatening the Amazon, the greed, lust, and hatred threatening its people.

One consequence of Western civilization's love affair with reason, according to Meunier and Savarin, is continuing violence against the Indians and their land. They find that "Indian and civilized cultures ... suffer from the same prejudice: it is the other who is the barbarian." In refutation, they cite Claude Lévi-Strauss's definition of barbarian: "a barbarian is a person who believes in barbarity."

With him, they find that "in Amazonia where the cult of manhood [*virilisme*] is king"[3] that women are used as a medium of exchange, a means of expression, "in which "men use women as the verbs by which they communicate with one another (men themselves are the nouns, of course)."[4] This "otherizing" of women is the oldest, the most basic oppression.

Yet Meunier and Savarin catch glimpses of a primal vision of men and women. Anthropology asks, "What is a human being?" and Meunier and Savarin answer with a "sentimental and speculative dream" of "Tenderness.

1. Jacques Meunier, *Le Monocle de Joseph Conrad* (Paris: La Découvert/Le Monde, 1987), 150. (My translations throughout.)
2. Meunier, 26.
3. Meunier, 32.
4. Robin Morgan, *The Word of a Woman* (New York: Norton, 1992) 89.

Mystery. Laughter."[5] Inspired by their own surrealist vision as well as by the stories and rituals of the Amazon tribes, their examination of cultural differences does not focus on "the familiarities and the unfamiliarities, on the neutral and the exotic," instead illuminating "the area in between—that fertile, liminal ground where new meanings germinate and where common experiences in different contexts can provoke new bonds."[6]

Their creation—at the same time a history and an anthropology book, a collection of exciting and disturbing stories, a poem, a polemic, a song of love and rage—is an "individual creation" like that of the tribal storyteller: a "myth dream ... unique, marginal, which can advance the group." And like a tribal myth, one would like to see it "repeated collectively.... linked dialectically (if I may use that term) to an ethos."[7] Because only this ethos of knowledge and compassion can lead to an end of the genocide in the Amazon.

The pressures of population and profit-driven capitalism have only gotten worse since the original publication of this book. The massacres of Amazon Indians continue, most recently with the brutal slaughter, by some accounts, of at least seventy-three Yanomami Indians (including thirty-four children and two pregnant women) by Brazilian miners near the Venezuelan border. Amid the public outcry that followed, Amnesty International reminded the world press that in sixteen previous incidents of Yanomami killings not a single murderer has ever been brought to trial.

Though their book has become a classic on its subject, Meunier and Savarin state in their preface to this edition that they are only glad that they contributed to a growing awareness of the problem. And surely the one faint hope for ending the genocide and restoring a healthy Amazonia is at the level of the individual. Noam Chomsky and others have recently argued that the best hope for the future lies not in institutions, in business or government, but the improvement of individual attitudes. In this argument we hear the echo of the attitudes of the primitive peoples for whom, despite their tribal values, each story is the unique expression of an individual sensibility. Marcos Terena, founder and president of the Union of Indigenous Nations of Brazil, has recently described the Amazonian people's

5. Meunier, 260.
6. Lucy R. Lippard, *Mixed Blessings* (New York: Pantheon, 1990), 9.
7. Meunier, 54–55.

quick realization that civilization was "fractured internally, because it had pushed to one side the very structure of natural man, of his spirit, of his soul." [8]

But as awareness builds to the critical mass that will bring about the revolution in consciousness, ecology, and economy that would make such violence impossible, the Amazonian rain forest and its Indians continue to disappear.

This story must be heard.

Carol Christensen
El Sobrante, 1993

8. Inter Press Service, *Story Earth: Native Voices on the Environment* (San Francisco: Mercury House, 1993), 37.

AUTHORS' PREFACE

WHEN WE CAME BACK from the Amazon, during the student demonstrations in May 1968, the streets of Paris came as no shock to us. We found that the city's explosive population bore a surprising resemblance to the primitive civilizations we had just left. This "revolution without a project" that swarmed from the Sorbonne to the Odéon, in the streets and bistros of the Latin Quarter, was just like the world of palaver and grand speeches, of direct democracy, of chiefs and followers, in short, just like the noises still ringing in our ears, the sounds of the people we had finally begun to know.

An illusion, perhaps. Still, that was what made us write this book instead of some other one. The words poured out of us in a steady stream, unstoppable, effortless. Everything we knew and everything we had seen went into it. Our 2CV Citroën became a traveling library.

The idea that we might be ruining our university careers by writing a book like this did not deter us. "Do nothing against your conscience even if the State demands it." Albert Einstein's words were our motto. And on rereading *The Amazonian Chronicles,* we have no regrets about taking the path that led us in a less "objective" direction....

It is no secret. There's little satisfaction in having been proved right. Better if the Amazonian Indians had been spared. Still, today's ethnologists cannot easily ignore what we have said; nor can the Indians, who have been faced with a second wave of the same kinds of killing and persecution and have started to organize. Without taking credit for any such improvement, we did feel that we contribute to it.

Because during the sixties, if there was a face-off between the right of civilizations and the rights of people to determine their fates, and if the right to interfere was not yet in style, the contact we made with this or that Amazonian Indian, sharing a meal of manioc or grilled monkey, in the house where our hammocks were slung, compelled us to get involved: in the name of the individual.

Our position, between science and outrage at science, did not warrant the attitude of our colleagues, the way our friends and other ethnologists looked down on our work. Except for Roger Bastide, Robert Jaulin, and Pierre Clastres. The latter provided this extremely perceptive observation: "Western reason always returns to a state of violence and to the use of violence, because it considers everything other than itself to be in a 'state of sin' and to fall into the horrifying realm of the unreasonable. And it is in light of this twin aspect of the West, its full image, that one must view its relation to primitive cultures: the actual violence of which they are victims is not separate from humanism, it is just the visible sign of reason carried to its farthest extreme; and under its mask, this twin aspect defines our culture. It seems that our culture can only organize itself in opposition to what it has defined as unreasonable."

Jacques Meunier & A. M. Savarin
Paris, 1991

The
Amazonian Chronicles

What Is an Indian?

WHAT IS AN
INDIAN?

"THE TUPINAMBA INDIANS clearly know nothing of enmity, of the greed, envy, and ambition that cause it or of the disputes and lawsuits that accompany it: of any of those vile, even pestilential, motives from which flows so much filth that poisons life in Europe and kills us before our time, gnawing our bones, sucking our marrow, eating away at our bodies, and consuming our spirits. Far from being inspired or ruled by any of these motives, they are completely untouched by them." The world portrayed in this description has become our model of an idyllic society. But in 1557, when it was written by Jean de Léry, there was little consensus about the nature of Indian society.

Physically, Indians are not all that different from us. They are not monsters: they are neither too large nor too small; they are strong and vigorous, without deformities; even old age does not impair them unduly. But this was not enough to convince a skeptical Europe of their humanity. In 1550, the city of Rouen organized a folklore festival at which fifty Indians from the region of Bahia, "savages, natives fresh from the country," along with two hundred fifty extras, sailors daubed with *urucu* and *genipa*,* constructed a camp on the banks of the Seine and displayed the art of living "without the least covering for the part governed by nature." This exotic festival had everything; Rouen's gawkers could even barter to obtain Indian goods, trading iron tools for parrots and monkeys, feathers and redwood. The finale was a staged battle between the Tupinamba and the Tabajara, a series of brutal clashes crowned by flurries of club blows, ending in the trouncing of the

---

* Urucu is a red vegetable dye; genipa, black.

Tabajara as flames leapt across the ramparts of the operetta fortress forming the backdrop. Henry II and Catherine de Médicis were delighted by the wild behavior of these new subjects; the chroniclers of the time do not tell us how the court ladies congratulated the true and the false savages, but they do note that "the eyes of the king were lit with satisfaction."

THE MYTH
OF THE
NOBLE SAVAGE

IT QUICKLY BECAME fashionable to reflect on the myth of the natural man. Montaigne had a servant who had been a *go-between;** he listened to the servant's tales and then wrote his essays describing a world that is without evil because it is without constraint. In Montaigne's view, even Plato had not conceived such a dream state: "How far from this perfection is the Republic that he imagined!" Ronsard, in his "Complaint against Fortune," was inspired by the woodcuts in Thevet's *Universal Cosmography* to depict natural man as a creature "who wanders innocently, completely wild,... and as free of clothing as he is of malice."

The idea of the noble savage remained alive through the eighteenth century in the Old World, where it served as the antithesis of Europe's corrupt society; but across the sea, the savages themselves were annihilated: in the New World, these poor unlettered creatures served as no more than tools for the new arrivals.

Apologists for the Indians multiplied, though with little effect: lawyers and other theoreticians had scant influence on soldiers of the crown. Few of the conquerors were as bad as the Pizarro brothers; other conquerors were not as cruel: Alvar Nuñez Cabeza de Vaca, for example, who was appointed governor of La Plata, tried to resist some of the Spanish demands and to protect the natives. Which was really no more than the appropriate gratitude: he had thought himself dead many times while crossing North

---

* An interpreter; a shipwreck survivor who had lived with the Indians for several years and had learned their language.

America on foot, from Florida to California; and he would never have made it out of that hell if he had not had the help of the Indians, who acted as his guides, relaying him across their lands. Then again, he may have had his own self-interest in mind, for his pro-Indian policy enabled him to collect generous gifts from the pacified populations. But at least he did not allow the officials who reported to him to use the harshest methods to resolve their problems. In the same spirit, in the seventeenth century, when the Quakers established their colony, William Penn went against tradition to propose that damages be paid to the Indians. His contemporaries saw this as terrible naïveté and suspected it was really just a dirty trick.

The conquerors of the New World had few scruples and but one desire: they dreamed of bounty, of acquiring riches quickly and easily. The Church worried about souls and the excesses of the conquistadore. Soon no expedition was allowed to sail without a missionary, to convert the populations of the new territories and to improve the morale of the armies. But these civilizers were completely lacking in ethnological sense and even had trouble making the infidels understand them. Consider this evidence, a comical exchange between the governor Pedrarias Dávila and the chronicler Fernandez de Oviedo:

> Sir, it seems to me that the Indians do not want to listen to the theological doctrine contained in the bishop's letter, and that you do not have anyone who can make them understand. Might Your Grace go so far in defense of this document as to give the order for us to throw a few of these Indians into prison, where they will be able to study the faith at their leisure, with Monsignor the Bishop to explain it to them.

If the pioneers saw the natives as a crew of slaves, the representatives of the good Catholic king and of Saint-Siège, in contrast, were determined to prevent all servitude, or at the very least to organize it to make it more efficient. In the first phase of the conquest, a few settlements were established along the coast; they controlled the adjacent land and were charged with exploiting this back country to the advantage of the mother country. In Brazil, expeditions were soon launched into the interior, in search of any and all salable goods. It is fortunate that the Portuguese administration did not choose to support any systematic transformation of these "excursions," or rather incursions into raids against the Indians. But how could these adventurers, with their own weapons and their own servants, be prevented from leaving the main body of the expedition to capture the slaves they needed?

"The number of people murdered in Bahia," wrote one Jesuit, "is unbelievable; one would not have thought it possible that so many people could have been killed in so short a time."

With the establishment of settlements and the development of projects for the conquest of the interior, it became more and more difficult to control the slave raids, the *descidas*. Playing upon a subtle distinction between slavery as a legal and as a natural institution, the Church followed the lead of the Jesuits to declare that this second form was appropriate to the case of the Indians, who were placed under guardianship. This subjugation of the Indians was the beginning of the *encomienda* system. The grantee and steward of an encomienda was not only given land but also was provided with a number of natives to work for him as forced laborers. In almost no time, this system, the South American version of slavery, succeeded in transforming the native population into a class of starving subhumans, wretched creatures who responded only to the whip and the rod and longed only for the death that would rescue them from suffering and disease. Bartolomé de Las Casas reports the last words of the Cuban Hatuey, a cacique condemned to execution for having tried to organize resistance to the Spanish: his oppressors offered him Paradise if he would convert *in articulo mortis;* he asked if he would have to associate with whites up above; when they answered yes, he declared that he would rather die a pagan.

Soon there was a shortage of manpower on the coast. Las Casas, the same priest who upheld Indian rights, suggested that black labor be imported. The advantages were obvious: blacks had already proved themselves as slaves, they were strong, and their use could save the Indians from complete decimation. In one stroke, Las Casas had invented the South American indigenous movement and the black slave trade.

Whatever the reality may have been, theoretically the Indian was not a slave but a serf. *The Laws of the Indies* were supposed to protect this status. It would be hard to say what the Indian gained from this new definition, exiled as he was in his own country.

Treated as overgrown children by the Jesuits, the Indians were subjected to a boarding-school regime that was intended to educate them. What should one make of this fabulous project, of this theocratic community where, under the direction of the good and quite thorough Fathers, adults returned to infancy were initiated into the art of living according to the

Western model? Organized into brigades, subjected to the most rigorous discipline, they learned to maintain and use European tools and to stumble their way through Christian doctrine; their course of study did not include Spanish, which was the language of their teachers; for the instruction of the disciples, a passe-partout idiom was created, most of it based on the Tupi language, the *lingua geral.*

This system of subjugation soon produced a docile population that eventually detribalized and settled into fixed communities; and, in fact, the Jesuits' policy is responsible for establishing at least a hundred villages. But the Indians? A native Peruvian chronicler, Guamán Poma de Ayala, gives a vivid description of the Indians' state at the end of the seventeenth century, the period of the conquest and establishment of the viceroyalty. Ayala was no defender of the virtues of the Spanish invaders: "After the Conquest, the bad example of the Spanish converted the Indians into shameless liars, drunkards, gamblers, and layabouts, wastrels who could not be trusted. They slept until lunchtime, they did not work their fields, they did not take care of their llamas; they did not gather guano to enrich their soil, firewood to cook their meals, or straw to repair the roofs of their houses; for them, life meant sleeping all day and doing nothing." Later he added, "The Indians abandoned their villages because the rulers, priests, and clergymen, the Spanish in general, kidnap their wives and daughters. When the father and mother protest, the Spanish take them by force, with the result that the Indians prefer to flee."

In Europe, a few decent and civilized men did speak out against the conquest. Thus, Lope de Vega wrote:

> So color de religion
> Van a buscar plata y oro
> Del incubierto tesoro.

[Under the banner of religion/ they go in search of gold and silver/ of hidden treasure.]

French philosophers used the theme of the conquest to denounce the vanity and cupidity of man. After careful consideration of the facts, Diderot found he was not able to accept the good faith of the men he called "cruel Spartans in black robes." (Were there any doubt of this assessment, it would be dispelled by an inventory of the wealth still held in the monasteries of certain Latin American countries.) All the Spanish representatives in America, religious or not, raked in gold and riches: "Only honest men, kind men, subjects who were full of sympathy and humanity," Diderot added ironically, "were sent by the European powers to govern their overseas possessions."

Condemnation of the civilized world for the crimes it committed against cultures it was pretending to assimilate, and for the cruel treatment to which it subjected defenseless Indians, led to further exaggeration of the virtues of primitive man, who became man as he should have been. Jean-Jacques Rousseau was no fool; he knew that his ideal state did not exist, that it probably never had and never would. Man is good; men are evil. The myth of the noble savage is only a myth. Most likely a memory of lost innocence and Bible stories. Paradise, the Fall, the babel of languages, these stories were all retold, translated into a strictly secular version by the author of *A Discourse on Inequality*. Socialist yet solicitous of man's dignity, to Voltaire's regret Rousseau did not go quite so far as to propose that people walk on all fours!

Chateaubriand took the popular stereotype of the Indian and added an exotic setting and a story tearful enough to melt the salons of Paris, thereby launching the indigenist literature that still has a hold over many aspiring Latin American revolutionaries.

General Cándido Rondon of Brazil was a positivist, a pacifist, and—an additional virtue—a man of action. Born in 1865, in Mimoso, a tiny village in the Mato Grosso, he was almost certainly part Indian. Defense of the Indians became his life's work, a project that was as dangerous as it was unusual. He has become one of Brazil's national heroes, credited with the exploration of the entire southwest section of his country. Creating detailed maps and covering the area with trails, he was also responsible for the installation of a telegraph system extending as far as the coast. "A Titanic labor," Theodore Roosevelt called it, "on the same scale as the construction of the Panama Canal." Among his accomplishments, he pacified thirteen tribes, among them the Xavantes, the Bororo, the Paressi, the Cabexi ... and he established the Service for the Protection of Indians. Around 1934, he saw his theories accepted; at the order of Getulio Vargas, an amendment was added to the national constitution recognizing his protégés' right to vast territories. Unfortunately, this was no more than a goodwill gesture; the law was never enforced. Few but its author lived up to Rondon's motto—Die if necessary; kill, never!—a motto that reflected his conviction that exotic communities could be integrated into our civilization slowly and peacefully. Today, the Villas-Boas brothers are attempting to carry on his work.

THE LEGEND OF
SILBACO

D ESPITE THE EFFORTS OF
a variety of organizations fired by pro-Indian sentiment, societies without
writing tend to disintegrate and disappear. Their passage from the traditional to the modern is painful. Ethnographers maintain that we are wit-
nessing these societies' final decline; these past ten years have seen the
extinction of more tribes than the previous forty. Soon there will be no more
Indians.

In fact, the Indians themselves are resigned; they view their demise as
fate, the tribute they owe to the powers above. Is this not, they ask, the end
that has been foretold for the only true men?

Fatalism is also the religion of the forests.... Their myths turn into perfect accomplices in the crimes of common law and genocide; they justify the
arrival of the whites: Cortés landing in Mexico could only be the emissary
of Quetzalcoatl, the plumed serpent whose return the natives awaited. The
Guarani Indian theology, too, had predicted the death of the tribe. Apart
from these pessimistic visions, a mythology also developed that foresaw a
return to a more just order. The codex of *Chilam Balam de Chumayel* contains
the promise of vengeance: "And there will come a day when the tears of the
Indians will reach God and all at once the justice of God will descend upon
the world. Someday the will of God will bring back Ah Kantenal, Yellow-
Altar-Spirit, and Ix Pucyola, Destroyer-of the Heart-of Water, to strike these
exploiters from the face of the earth."

In the second half of the nineteenth century, the period in which the
exploitation of the Rio Negro region intensified, Brazilian "patrons" forced
the Indians to work without pay.

This escalation of colonialism favored the return of the messianic illusion, which produced "Indian Christs," who exhorted their disciples to abandon their work and drink and flagellate themselves until they fell to the ground in a trance. These visionaries incited the oppressed Indians to rise up against the whites. One of them, a shaman or sorcerer from the Araposo tribe, claimed that he was the "father of the missionaries," and that since he was responsible for their coming, he knew best how to get rid of them. All prophesied the reversal of the racial order: whites would soon be the slaves, *their* slaves. The Tikuna Indians rose up several times in revolts of this type and—although we lack any more recent information—we know that these movements were still active in 1950.

In the beginning, these xenophobic crusades, which were fired by a desire for freedom as well as this profane interpretation of Christianity, always followed the same pattern: first, spirits appeared to an adolescent, telling him about the future, describing a day of wrath and vengeance. It would be the end of the world and of the whites. But, according to the prophecy, the Indians belonging to the tribe would escape if they performed a complicated ritual: while awaiting the deluge, they were to construct a huge communal hut; taking refuge in it, they were to offer thanks to the spirits for having given them warning.

The legend of Silbaco expresses the same desire for revolt, but in a less mystical form; it is a more naïve tale, inspired by both the Guarani Indian myth of the Urutau and the cheap romances of the jungle traders. Silbaco, the Ay Ay Mama of the forests of the Ucayali, is a nightjar, a bird that sings a sorrowful tune; its brooding and mournful voice troubles the darkening hour of dusk. Here is a version told to us by a rubber tapper on the banks of the Guaporé River:

Huari was the son of Iguaso, the cacique of the Tumacos. He was beautiful, young, and strong. When his father died, he would become the head of the clan.

One day he was out on a hunt. He was far from his camp when he met a group of whites who attacked him, leaving him seriously wounded. Nearly mad with pain, he was praying for death, when suddenly he heard the sound of footsteps. Oh miracle! A bright shadow stepped out from between the trees. It was a girl with long golden hair. Never had Huari seen such beauty. The unknown girl came closer to him and gestured; immediately two hunters appeared, picked up Huari, and carried him deep into the forest.

Huari stayed for some time with the tribe of Nihuana, the fair Indian girl. One day, he said to her, "Now I have to return to my own people." At these words, the eyes of the wild woman grew wet with tears. "Oh, Nihuana, you love me!" Huari took her in his arms and they exchanged their first kiss.... Huari no longer dreamt of leaving. He was the most tender of lovers. Nothing was too good for his beloved: the beautiful feathers of toucans and blue partridges, magical plants "to make one's insides strong." They were the envy of all the other couples.

But bad luck was lying in wait for them. The Karajana, the white men, who were said to be more ferocious than pumas, were sowing terror far beyond their own lands. The Indians were putting up a desperate fight in defense of their territory. Huari took part in all the battles. Courageous and bold, he seemed to laugh at the white peril, and finally he was struck down by fate: he sank to the ground under a hail of bullets. His last thoughts were for Nihuana.

Nihuana did not want to believe that her lover was dead, and even when his companions stood before her bearing his dead body, she refused to accept her misfortune. She moaned, she wept. No one could quiet her tears. She swore to avenge him. So strong was her hatred, so powerful her will, so terrible were the curses she uttered that her soul departed her body. The glade was bathed in a strange light, and the ball of fire that had been her soul took the form of a fantastic bird, black as a night of tempest and terror....

Ever since this time, Silbaco has haunted the forests. It is the condemned soul of what used to be the beautiful Nihuana. It lingers in deserted places, frightening travelers; it never tires of repeating its message: over and over it sings of the end of the white masters, the Karajana.

It is full of meaning, this story in which the victims console themselves by imagining the end of their oppressors, with a mythic bird as their only weapon. For civilized man, tools of destruction; for primitives, language. The soliloquys of an entire people. Proud and shy, the indigenous cultures do not accept the outsider speaking to them, no matter who he may be; they remain turned in upon themselves, denying the superiority of Western civilization. Indian and civilized cultures, we can see, suffer from the same prejudice: it is the other who is the barbarian.

THE MYTH OF THE
BAD INDIAN

A POWER WISHING TO
colonize and control will go to any lengths to justify illegitimate acts,
including the act of sequestering the savages in their savagery. The myth of
the bad Indian—less familiar than its double, but more diabolical and obviously more useful—has given rise to many a misdeed. The law of supply
and demand produced a fair number of chroniclers who were ready to satisfy this need: in 1622, for example, there appeared in Venice a portrait
claiming to represent a native of Brazil. It was unquestionably monstrous.
Looking at it more closely, one became aware that the artist had not been
burdened with an excess of scientific rigor. He had copied the dog-man of
Pliny!

In the first years of the conquest, Villegaignon was scandalized that his
men could "go and debauch with savage women." Infuriated by this laxity
of morals, he did not hide his scorn for the indigenous populations; "these
irrational beasts" must be kept away from the men in his troop.

Then, too, Indians inspired fear. The difficulties encountered by the Europeans when they attempted to penetrate Brazil's interior made them "suspect
that the natives had fortified the mountains to prevent access to them," to
quote the chronicler Simão de Vasconcelos. There was no lack of men who
believed that Indians were the devil's children and that they served only the
devil; after all, they stood in the way of the conquest and resisted the efforts
of the Jesuits, who wanted to set up their own camps in subjugated areas.

Harassed, hounded, and destroyed by lies and disease, the Indian remained a mysterious and disturbing creature. It began to seem necessary
to provide reasons for finding him so troubling. One could allege, with

Benjamin Franklin, that "Divine Providence intended to eliminate these savages in order to give the land to men who would cultivate it." Certainly, it is more comfortable to find the Indian himself responsible for his sorry fate, by making him the incarnation of nearly all the vices and depicting him without any redeeming qualities. At the end of the eighteenth century, there was a guide published in Madrid for the use of travelers who wanted to go from Buenos Aires to Lima. Its author, no doubt a half-caste Peruvian, paints an unflattering portrait of the natives he has encountered: filthy, lazy, two-faced.... He concludes that the Black Legend of the Spanish conquistadores might not be as accurate as the missionaries would have one believe.

The conquerors went so far as to make lists of the Indians' bad qualities, the traits that made the conquerors so eager to exterminate them; the most comprehensive was probably that of Enrique Lopez Albujar, who summarized: "The Indian is hypocritical, submissive, defiant, false, selfish, venal, negligent, sordid." German ethnologist Günther Tessmann passed judgment in these words: "One cannot do the Indian any good, because that will make him worse; one cannot do him any evil, because charity will not allow it."

This completely negative image of the Indian is a little too summary. Let us be fair to Lopez Albujar. If his indictment is pitiless, he later tries to amend it, offering the following, more judicious statement: "The Indian is a sphinx with two faces: indifferent to the future, he has one face turned toward the past; the other, toward the present. The first he uses to live among his own people; the second, to communicate with strangers."

The beginning of the twentieth century favored these imaginary representations—exoticism was a big hit. The period before the war saw a new explosion of reason; and, as everyone knows, the return of monsters was greeted with applause.... People swarmed to Luna Park, the aging Barnum and Bailey had a new triumph, *Freaks* was filmed, and—oh, how naïvely—the stage was set for Hiroshima. Primitive man became a spectacle. The *Journal des voyageurs* could not carry this mood of excess any farther; journalists took up the ancient themes, embellished them, and, with any talent, made their fortune repeating the same exotic curiosities. Their teratology—the science of monsters—was fraudulently presented as anthropology. Here are some of the images they gave of South American natives: the irreducible dwarfs of Federmann—their height: thirty-three inches! the crab-men, the tribe of Amazons, the Pita Yavai (their feet reversed), the headless men, the blond Indians ... and a whole fabulous collection of unnatural animals and not-quite-men.

Then, the Western film made massacre its favorite activity: proof that the civilized conscience was not troubled by the genocide of the Indian. Our vocabulary still reveals the mark of a certain contempt; note the terms that insult the Huron, the Apache, the Aztec. In South America, a furious taxi driver, held up by a parade of students walking single file, will yell out "Indians!" Falsified images. Images that cannot be separated from the tragedy of the race, images that must be dispelled. Scientific types listen in on exotic cultures, and what they set out to discover, however banal this may become from day to day, is the price of a life dominated by a precarious and elusive agreement between man and nature. Whether the primitive group is object of study or subject for thought, every discourse about it strives to clarify one theme, one question whose answer always seems to elude us: what does it mean to be human?

The Indian, rediscovered by the scientist, helps us to better understand humanity as well as to weigh the relative value of our own culture: the Indian way of "being human" is as good as any, as good as every way, and that is why it is no small matter to carry on the effort to collect the experience—irreversible and irreplaceable—of all the peoples we call primitive.

Can one avoid the trap of both these exoticisms? Henri Michaux manages in these lines:

> Trapus, brachycéphales, à petits pas,
> Lourdement chargés marchent les Indiens
> Dans cette ville, collée dans un cratère de nuages.
> Où va-t-il, ce pèlerinage voûte?
> Il se croise et s'entrecroise et monte; rien de plus;
> C'est la vie quotidienne.

[Thick-bodied, big-headed, with tiny steps/ the Indians carry terrible burdens/ through this village sunk in a crater of clouds./ Where does it lead, this vaulted pilgrimage?/ It crosses and recrosses and travels higher; nothing more;/ it is daily life.]

But between the extravagant and the ordinary, the image of the Indian has not yet found a genius grand enough to convey it simply.

And what of Amazonia?

PART ONE

A New World

THE GREEN HELL
OF LITERATURE

Long before we explore Amazonia, we believe in the existence of rich and fantastic countries. The infernal host of trees, ramparts of sand, black-lead haze. We see this forest long before we enter it, slipping into the green cameo of its scenery. Our canoists mumble a litany in time with their strokes; we move past the settled zones, the huge ranches with their imported cows and their zebus, their horses running free, and soon we enter the most Gothic of all the forests. Here dwells lyricism. We invent Amazonia! Much later, travelers reveal it to us.

Amazonia? Water and a lot of trees ... four million square miles. As that does not impress us, they add: more than a thousand tributaries feed the same river, seventy-nine billion gallons of water per hour near its mouth, eight thousand kinds of trees on its banks. A fifth of all the fresh water on the planet flows there; a quarter of all the trees in the world grow there. We still do not say a word. A little irritated, they throw out a rush of details in an extravagant inventory: the boas there reach fify-two and one-half feet long, the piranhas fifteen feet, there are more than seven hundred types of butterflies, the water lilies measure six and one-half feet around; and everything, everything is on the same grand scale. Two of the tributaries of the Amazon are more important than the Rhine, seven are more than nine hundred miles long. The river system seems to mock the fundamental laws of geography; the Orinoco has an arm that flows into the Amazon, the Purus River flows out of this ocean-river and then rejoins it some ninety-three miles later. Several entire islands, huge masses of water hyacinths drift gently with the current.... We have stopped listening. In truth, we are not moved by figures. For us, Amazonia is less an area than an element, an atmosphere. H. M. Tomlinson was right when he wrote, "The mind sees the forest more clearly than the eyes."

As a literary image, the forest is clearly related to the grotto and the cathedral. It transfigures sounds, refracts light, suffuses us with perfumes blended of ferns and dead bodies. Land of shadow, of reflections; no sky, no horizon, no seasons. Primordial forest, taken to the farthest limits, and peopled with all the demons of our childhood terrors. Closed world, immense cathedral that rejects man as much as it imprisons him. "You have robbed me of the dream of the horizon and have left my eyes with only the monotony of your zenith, above which unfurls a tranquil dawn that never brightens the dead leaves of your damp caverns. You are the cathedral of regret, where the unknown gods speak whisperingly in the language of murmurs, promising long life to the towering trees, contemporaries of paradise."*

Here, it is proper (and inescapable) to quote François-René de Chateaubriand: "The forests were the first temples of the divinity, and they gave man his first ideas of architecture.... These vaults chiseled of foliage, these jambs that support the walls and terminate abruptly in broken trunks, the brilliance of the heights, the shadows of the sanctuary, the long dark aisles, the secret passages, the low doors, the labyrinths of the woods, all these call to mind the gothic church: all make us feel a religious terror, the mysteries of the divinity."

It is not surprising that people have sought the road to the Promised Land there. Never before had it seemed so close at hand, when, on his third voyage, in 1498, Christopher Columbus landed on the island of Trinidad, determined his position from Ptolemy's map, and confidently announced that the Orinoco was the river that flowed from Paradise. From the very beginning, the Spanish captains who traveled to the New World to harvest gold and souls were anxious to locate the kingdom of Eldorado there. In the seventeenth century, Father Antonio de Leon Pinelo advanced the argument—irrefutable, he claimed—that this new land must be a part of the Garden of Eden. But as expedition followed expedition, despite hopes that the city of the Caesars had been founded there—a marvelous oasis deep in Patagonia, in Trapalandia—Paradise was not found on the new continent.

---

* José Eustachio Rivera.

A GRAND BOTANICAL GARDEN

Instead of miraculous countries, the *condottieri* found insects and swamps and fish that devoured livestock; they encountered poisons and strangling vines and a welter of other nightmares. Only scholars and naturalists were able to profit from the place. And, since the term *discovery* applies to territories where exploration is accompanied by the acquisition of knowledge of their true nature, it is to these scientists that we owe the discovery of America. They drew America from the realm of fantasy by moving systematically and methodically to map its frontiers.

On 16 May 1735, Charles Marie de la Condamine left the port of La Rochelle at the head of an expedition sponsored by the Academy of Sciences to establish the meridian of Quito and verify the shape of the earth. If eight years later the group was able to write *The arc is measured!* It was as much due to obstinacy as to scientific talent. Ridiculous conflicts with the local authorities, endless deliberations, friction among the members of the expedition, not to mention the illness and death of several of the company and the desertion of others. After these eight years, a trip down the Amazon seemed no more than a Sunday outing. It took two months for this company to reach the coast under the leadership of an Ecuadorian named Maldonado. It is to La Condamine that we owe a detailed map of the Amazonian basin, a number of plant collections, notable for their inclusion of rubber and quinine bark, and, most important, his published notes on the trip, the observations of a man of good sense and true science.

Very few people are familiar with the eight volumes of *Voyages dans l'Amérique meridionale* by Alcide d'Orbigny, published in Paris between 1835 and 1847. This is a great pity, since these books form an extraordinary document, a botanical, mineralogical, zoological, and entomological encyclopedia. Presenting the results of eight years of research in Uruguay, in Patagonia, and especially in Bolivia, d'Orbigny produced such a lavish work that the complete set, illustrated with numerous hand-drawn plates, cost five thousand dollars, an exorbitant price even today.

As for Baron Alexander von Humboldt (1769–1859), his influence was so great that Simón Bolívar could say that the baron "had done more for America than all the conquistadores." Inspired by his reading of La Condamine, he embarked for Venezuela in 1798, accompanied by the French doctor and botanist Aimé Bonpland. He traveled up the Orinoco to the Rio Negro and then the Magdalena; from Bogota, he went to Quito and made the climb up

Mount Chimborazo, thought at the time to be the highest mountain in the world. Then he went to Lima, sailing to Mexico from there. Humboldt returned to Europe in 1804, but not before traveling to Cuba and the United States. He took back detailed collections of plants, insects, and geological samples and spent the rest of his life drafting the twenty-nine volumes that comprise his complete works, all of which can still be consulted with perfect confidence.

If H. M. Tomlinson (born in London in 1873) is almost entirely unknown, it may be because he had nothing to do with the academies of higher learning. He was a reporter for a daily newspaper in London. One day he got an urge to board a freighter that was carrying a load of coal to a port near the mouth of the Amazon. He was not a scholar, he was not part of any university clique, but he wrote a book about his trip, *The Sea and the Jungle,* that is the first book about Brazil to provide a glimpse of the intimacy of the forest, the furious life that animates it.

These are only a few names, a few notables from a very long list that would have to include Paul Lecointe, Georges de Créqui-Monfort, Richard Spruce, Jules Crevaux, and all those who surveyed Amazonia, gathering plants and picking up pebbles and adventures, collecting beasts and flowers and fables.... Despite their efforts, Amazonia has not cast off its legend. It is still a tremendous collector of stories and strange beings, the sacred land of science fiction; difficult as it may be to accept, the fact is that no matter how realistically we view the Amazon, it will still find countless ways to astonish us.

PIRANHAS! PIRANHAS!

An anthology of Amazonian motifs, that is what is needed, a collection of key images, of vital words, the ones that give the Amazonian space its power of seduction, the ones that call up our dreams. The project of a lifetime. The Amazon, where we meet the animals of our first picture alphabets: the cayman, the jaguar, the parrot, the monkey, and those others....

Prognathous jaws, round eyes, the first thing they show us is their cruelty. Frenzied fish. They are the absolute enemies of life, of everything that moves. Blood drives them crazy, and noise; their thirty-six thousand traps snap shut on the tiniest animalcule. Squadrons of death. Piranhas! Piranhas! Piranhas!

"A member of an American expedition traveling up the Chaco River fell asleep and left his hand dangling in the river. His hand was attacked and the flesh stripped from it before he awoke. The shock he felt upon seeing his hand reduced to a skeleton made him faint and he tumbled into the river. The current was so strong that his companions were unable to fish him out immediately. When they managed to reach him, only a few minutes later, there was nothing left of him but his bones and his clothes." If Creation were ever put on trial, there is one decision that would be overwhelming: beyond a shadow of a doubt, these assassins would be sentenced to an eternal fast. The incident above was reported by Willard Price in a book titled, with painful irony, *Marvels of the Amazon!*

Personally, we have encountered three types of piranhas. One is light-colored, about four inches long, one has a red belly, and one is predominantly black, about ten inches long. They are all edible. But for amateur fishermen, our advice would be to string the pole with piano wire and use triple-strength fishhooks; attract the fish by flicking a finger on the surface of the water a few times.... The Indians, who like to eat piranha meat, have nevertheless made them into the "the justice of the lagoons." These piranhas, called *buiogoé* by the Bororo, exhibit behavior the hero of mythology has chosen to suppress. Cannibalistic, castrating spirits, they occupy an accessory position in the world of the savage imagination; at least, they do not inspire as much commentary as in literate societies. The theme of the "vagina dentata" represents the most spectacular manifestation of their evil reputation. Private property has its guard dogs; savagery, its piranhas of chastity.

THE BOA AND THE RAINBOW

To the dazzling blind aggression of a piranha strike the popular imagination opposes the long, slow digestive process of the anaconda and the boa constrictor. They slip from the literal to the figurative sense, from the alimentary to the sexual, playing with language like a living poem. For native peoples, the anaconda *knows* its victims. It *assimilates* them; no doubt this explains why they place the snake under the double sign of death and fertility.

Referring to Cobacchini, Claude Lévi-Strauss tells the Bororo myth "The Origin of Tobacco":

The men were coming back from hunting and they whistled, the way they always did, to call their women to come meet them and help them carry the game.

So it was that a woman named Aturuaroddo was carrying a piece of a boa snake that her husband had killed; the blood that flowed from its flesh penetrated her body and made her pregnant.

This "son of the blood" spoke to his mother while still in her womb. He suggested that he might help her to harvest wild fruit. In the form of a snake, her son left her body, slithered up a tree, and picked all the fruit, throwing it down for his mother to gather. The mother tried to flee, but the serpent caught her and crawled back into her empty uterus.

The horrified woman confided in her elder brothers, who set a trap for the son. No sooner had the serpent gone from her to climb the tree, than the mother ran off; and when it slid back down the tree to reenter her body, the brothers killed it.

The men put the snake's body on a funeral pyre to burn, and from the ashes were born urucu, the resin tree, tobacco, corn, and cotton.

In the Peruvian Amazon, among the Ocaina, the boa is a no less incredible figure:

First, there was Amena Kogoen; she was a young girl, a virgin, very pretty, but her parents had kept a close watch on her since she was very small. She lived a quiet life with them.

One day, Noi Mura, a boa who had the power to change into a man, sneaked into her house through a hole in the floor. He taught her to be a woman.

The seducer returned several times; he brought Amena Kogoen many presents and nice things to eat. Their lovemaking gave them all the more pleasure for being secret. No one would have suspected if the girl had not started to get big....

The girl's mother recognized her daughter's condition and found the hole in the floorboard of the hut. Guessing the trick, she poured boiling water into it and killed the serpent.

One night the spirit of the serpent appeared to the young girl:

"You are carrying my son in your belly; give birth to him in the little valley and leave him there. I love you, I will bring you many good things to eat; but I will kill your mother."

She gave birth to a boy and left him in the little valley, as her dead lover had said. Four days later, she returned to see her son, and in his place she found a beautiful tree, such as had never been seen before. The tree quickly grew tall, and its huge branches were soon covered with all the fruits necessary for human life: sweet and bitter manioc, corn, *makamo*, groundnuts, etcetera.

These savages—in the etymological sense of the term, *people of the forest* have been inspired by the millenary company of nature to develop a logic that strives to transpose reality, and it is for this reason that sorcerers are so powerful among them. Thus, among the Huitoto, the anaconda is the guardian of all waters, and the serpent's link with meteorological phenomena is expressed in the name of the rainmaker, Aima, and that of Buinaima, the storm god; there is one and only one man who can mediate these forces, the shaman, who commands the rain: "I give the order to unloose the rainfall, and the serpent obeys me."

As for Nuzo, the rainbow, this is a serpent that is so big and so strong that the Indians dare not even point a finger at it, for fear of its cruel bite. That is why the Huitoto usually indicate a rainbow by a motion of the elbow. Among the Cocama, the Indians say that rain is only the urine of *Mui Waso*, the sky snake, and they pray he will demonstrate his goodwill to fertilize their fields.

They are beneficent, then, these boas, and play a special, even central, role in the indigenous cosmogeny, in agrarian rites; so it is not too surprising that they are often represented, using rhomboid or triangular marks, on painted faces, pottery, and woven fabrics.

For the other inhabitants of the Amazon, both creoles and mestizos, the giant ophidians are the subject of long discussions in the course of which the monsters grow by several feet. A man who lived alongside the Napo River told us that one time a giant boa decided to take up residence in the lagoon that bordered his father's *chacra*.* Of course, he could not say exactly how big it was, but the animal "was at least forty yards long and weighed at least four or five tons." And, he added, "My father, who was quite smart, quickly figured out a way to get rid of it. He threw some chunks of broken

* Cleared and cultivated land.

glass into the lake. That way, you see, the serpent could not come and sleep there; and it was never seen again."

The truth is that there are some very large serpents; Algot Lange tells us that in New York there is a dried skin measuring about fifty-two and one-half feet long by about five feet around. Colonel Fawcett and Blaise Cendrars saw one of quite respectable size. The anaconda, a semiaquatic and semiarboreal serpent, is the largest of the boas; still, it only rarely reaches forty feet. The boa constrictor, a more familiar animal, is also smaller (seldom more than eleven and one-half feet); farmers sometimes tame them in order to control rats and mice.

Animals far less noble than the anaconda and the boa of the Indian myths fill the white man's stories of Amazonia. Every size and type, they have one thing in common, a devious attack: venomous snakes, electric fish, spiders, not to mention the most awful of them all, that horrible tormenting enemy, the mosquito. The forest raises a squadron of defenses against the intruder. Snares and traps protect its access. Only the Indians move through the jungle unharmed, and they too seem to be guardians of this incomprehensible order. They know its plants and they know how to procure its most potent poisons.

CURARE: A CHEMICAL WEAPON

"Ever since the fall from paradise, the entire human race has been infected by the foul and fatal poison of the infernal serpent, but the vile creature is still not satisfied. It has neither exhausted nor renounced its malignity and continues spewing forth new deaths: killing souls with sin, bodies with the poisons it offers to men of reason and judgment; and with the hidden poisons that it discovered and disclosed to the blind tribes of the Orinoco and similar places." So begins the treatise Father José Gumila dedicated to "that deadly poison called *curare.*"

The conquerors had told their tales of traveling through Venezuela, Colombia, and the Chaco, and seeing their companions drop down dead, victims of the dread *hervoladas* arrows, arrows that had been dipped in vegetable poisons. Since then, all sorts of fables have grown up around this infallible weapon; curare has quite naturally found its place in the phantasmagoria of the spinners of adventure tales. Curare must surely be blended from the thousand ingredients of traditional sorcery, combined with vapors so foul that they invariably kill the old hags charged with preparing them; if by some miracle a wounded man survives the convulsions brought on by the poison, he will find that his virility has been permanently destroyed.

It may be magic to the Europeans, but to the Indians curare is just a chemical weapon used by hunters. They say that a man once saw a falcon sinking its talons into the bark of a vine before pouncing on its prey; the hunter poked his arrows into the vine and the animals he shot collapsed, paralyzed; ever since that time the Indians have prepared curare to coat the tips of the tiny arrows they use in their blowpipes. The method of preparation is important. Curare is always prepared by a man, who determines the power of the ointment by carefully following the recipe:

> Gather some Strychnos vines; grate the bark to obtain about six and one-half pounds of scrapings; combine with an equal volume of water; place over a roaring Wre; bring to a boil and let simmer for twelve hours. Prepare another two pounds of grated bark and add it to the syrup obtained in the Wrst procedure; simmer this mixture for another twelve hours. Combine this with palm leaves and Piperacees wood, which have Wrst been chopped and crushed. The resulting mixture should look like pitch and have a similar consistency; it should not be too light, or it will not be strong enough. In the proper concentration, it will bring down a toad before the animal can take three jumps.

Like all recipes, this one has local variations. Depending on the region, either the *Strychnos* or the *Chondodendron* vine is used. The Kagua add to their mixture the crushed teeth or skulls of poisonous snakes, plus pimentos and large ants. The Nambikwara use a potion of pure *Strychnos*. But most of the "curare masters" combine their preparations with bits of Piperacees wood, which causes coagulation, and therefore prevents the poison from draining out of the wound.

First discovered by the Indians of the Amazon and the Guyana plateau, curare is also used by the Carib and Arawak tribes, who rub it on the tips of the arrows they shoot from large bows. It is an important trade good and certain tribes are reputed to have the best "crush"; the Piaroa and the Tikuna, especially, have made it their principal medium of exchange.

But, contrary to what Western stories might lead one to believe, curare has never been used in warfare. At most it may have been used in a few desperate situations, when the alternative was extermination. This was probably true when the whites arrived; there is no way to be sure, since curare victims die an agonizing death within twenty-four hours. Curare is not a poison that kills slowly. Perhaps Westerners confused it with other poisons. Or blood poisoning. In any case, curare use is strictly controlled; it cannot be used against men, or only in extremely rare circumstances. It took the imagination of civilized man to see it as the tool for the perfect murder—silent and lethal, it is the perfect weapon for the heroes in detective novels. The curare master has no such secret motives as he watches the pots where "the-death-that-kills-all-below" is bubbling and boiling.

The white man, nevertheless, has discovered indispensable drugs among the Indians' vegetable poisons. Amazonian traders still eagerly seek curare, but now it is to sell to distant laboratories. Each year, around nine hundred pounds of curare are shipped from Iquitos to the United States. It is used in anesthesia, when the doctor wants the patient to be completely immobilized, but still conscious and alert. Thanks to curare, the nerve-muscle connection is cut and the patient becomes the object of a remarkable "physiological autopsy" performed by the surgeon. Distant cousins to the Piaroa chemists, these surgeons have depoeticized curare; they have reduced it to a mere formula: $C_{40}H_{50}O_2N_4$. Then there are the other drugs: *mancenillier* (*Hippomane Mancenilla L.*), a small tree found on sandy beaches, so deadly even its shadow will kill a man—the Lacandon Indians take some of its *chechem,* extracting its sap to use on their arrows; it causes dramatic symptoms of photosensitization, characterized by edema, violent erythema, and raging fevers. And there is *barbasco,* a vine used by fishermen; placed in the water, it paralyzes the fish, who float to the surface belly-up, and into the weirs stretched out to catch them. And *ayahuasca,* the hallucinogen used in ritual ceremonies.... Doctors and hippies comb the forests in search of a miracle drug that will cure cancer, ensure eternal youth, or produce extraordinary visions.

TO MAKE A SHRUNKEN HEAD...

Ambiguous plants; drugs that can kill or lead to an artificial paradise, depending on how they are used; treacherous or ferocious animals— nothing escapes the Amazon's avid tourists, the twentieth century's banal voyeurs and explorers. To a curious world frantically searching for the bizarre, the Amazon seems like a gift from the gods. And for the man who is in too much of a hurry to add this extra kink to his itinerary, there is still hope! The tourist agency will certainly be able to take him to the nearest Oriental bazaar, where he will find heaps of the unlikeliest odds and ends, among them a few "trophies" captured from the Indians of the *Oriente* (the term refers to the eastern part of the country, which might as well be the end of the world): their pottery, fabrics, weapons, jewels, gris-gris, real or false, whatever is startling, primitive. And what could be more unusual than a little brownish shrunken head, not much bigger than a fist, topped with a bristling shock of black hair? Likely as not these shrunken heads are fakes, made of goatskin or monkey heads or god knows what. Bah! Just do not look at them too closely; too bad the Jivaro do not mass-produce them. In fact, it is practically impossible to find an authentic shrunken head, or *tzanta* (after two years in South America, we finally found two for sale at the Hotel Drouot, priced at seventy thousand old francs). The Jivaro still shrink heads, in a very long ceremony, using heads taken from rival tribes; but it occurs very rarely and is illegal nowadays. (In Ecuador, owning or transporting a tzanta is punishable by two years in prison.) Tzantas are not merely art objects: in removing the skin from the skull and then tanning it and recreating a head with the lips and the eyelids sewn tight, the Jivaro permanently neutralize the power of their enemy and his spirit. This process must be completed outside the village: the trophy prepared, they knead the leather filled with warm sand until the face begins to emerge again. It takes nearly five days to turn a severed head into a tzanta, an object that can safely be taken home.

WE GRINGOS

From Quito, it is easy to go and visit the Jivaro. No trouble at all to arrange transportation, lodging, guide; the whole trip is carefully planned, even— and most of all—the excursion to view the horrible headshrinkers. Ritual dances, souvenirs, the full show. But if this program seems tame, if the traveler prefers stronger sensations, it is still possible to tease out an adventure and go a little farther. As a reward, one may find the savages camping alongside a lake, no tourist stand, no transistors. The infernal paradise of the *gringos*. The forest has a horror of man in general, and of the gringo in particular. The gringo, that is the "paleface," or, more precisely, the Anglo-Saxon with his explorer's costume, his pidgin Spanish, and, especially, his amazing gift for attracting disasters, getting lost two steps from the village, tangled up in vines, tripping over rocks, tipping over his canoe, and coming back with a face swollen by mosquito bites. The feeblest sort of man. Whether he is wearing a camera or a crucifix around his neck, he has his fixed ideas, his quirks, but the courage he shows in doing so many useless things almost makes him sympathetic. He wants us to get undressed, we get undressed. He wants us to kneel down, we kneel down. But the saddle starts to pinch when he tries to get us to exchange our feather headdresses for some mirrors made in Japan! Our headdresses go for fifty dollars in Lima....

Travelers do not think, they remember. The most innocent prose, the most lively, like the recital of some odyssey, can conceal its weight of crime, or acceptance of the worst. We ask our readers to weigh words, and not succumb to the temptation of the picturesque. Primitive man is not a spectacle. Lévi-Strauss has said it and we will say it again: *barbarian* has a strict definition—and one that applies to both primitive and civilized societies—a barbarian is a person who believes in barbarity.

AMAZONIA, FROM
ORELLANA TO
BRASILIA

GREATDISCOVERIES

DID CHRISTOPHER COLUMBUS
invent the world of the Americas? Or did John Cabot reach it before him?
And Jean Cousin, from Dieppe, didn't he first see the Amazon in 1488? And
the English seamen looking for new fishing grounds? Whatever his role, the
Genoan believed steadfastly in his western Indies; the space between Europe
and Asia shrank, became riddled with islands, but the fourth continent had
not yet been *recognized*. While the new lands simply appeared, the discovery
needed to be established. In 1503, Amerigo Vespucci published an account
of his expedition: "It is right to call it a New World, because none of these
regions was known to our ancestors. I have discovered a vast continent
there." The West was accustomed to seeing geography revise its atlas, and,
in 1507, a mapmaker named Martin Waldseemüller detached a mass from
Asia, sketching in its outlines and christening it *America*. The new world
wailed as it was plunged into the Atlantic. It had yet to be examined.

In the first years of the conquest, the New World was enclosed, its coasts
occupied. The Spanish commandos mounted an assault on the Andes. The
expedition balked at the jungle. When Pizarro had pillaged the Inca Empire,
he sent his brother Gonzalo to search for mysterious lands: Eldorado, the
land of cinnamon and spices, and perhaps a passage to the Atlantic. In
February 1541, Gonzalo Pizarro, with Francisco de Orellana as his second,
found himself at the head of a fantastic convoy: two hundred ten Spaniards,
horsemen and foot soldiers; four thousand Indians, men and women; four or

five thousand pigs, a thousand dogs, and a herd of llamas. In August 1542, they returned to Quito: they had eaten their pigs, their llamas, their horses, and their dogs, and not one of the Indians was left alive. Orellana had taken a detachment down the river and had not returned. Survivors had seen traces of a camp at the confluence of the Napo and another large river and had waited there for several days, until hunger forced them to turn back.

Nevertheless, a month later, Orellana and his men arrived on the Atlantic coast. They had undergone such terrible hardships that they had not had the strength to fight the current and return to Pizarro; then, by chance, they had been carried away on the ocean-stream, where they had had a series of remarkable adventures. Not least of which was their encounter with a band of fierce Amazons, recounted in the chronicle of their expedition written by Father Gaspar de Carvajal, a description swarming with epic details: "These women are very white and very large. They wear their hair very long and braided or coiled around their heads. They are very robust and go entirely naked, except for their private parts, which are covered. They carry a bow and arrows and they fight like ten Indians." He was probably describing the Yagua Indians, who wear nothing but loincloths and have long manes even today, but the Amazons bestowed their name on a river that one of Columbus's companions, Vincente Yanez Pinson, had already named the Santa Maria de la Mar Dulce.

The "splendid land of the Amazon" was thoroughly inhospitable: with its rains, its floods, its swamps, it had reduced the proud conquerors to a pack of frustrated old soldiers. The "cinnamon trees" were worthless plants; Eldorado could not be located; even torturing the Indians did not yield any information about it. And as for proving the river link between the Pacific and the Atlantic, that could be no more than a dream, travel in the area was so hazardous.

Several years later Andrés Hurtado de Mendoza, viceroy of Peru, tried to discover a less dangerous route. The Spanish soldiers found their situation unendurable. Panic, desertions, rebellions, followed by the assassination of their leader Pedro de Ursua. He was quickly replaced, by a leader whose extremes of harshness and cruelty were enough to take them all the way to the mouth of Amazon. An amazing feat, leaving us with the memory of an adventure that was tragic, bloody, and ultimately rather glorious.

From then on, there were only a few sporadic and small-scale attempts to explore the jungle. But when the soldiers with their harquebuses abandoned the jungle, they were replaced by the missionaries. Especially, the Jesuits. Bit by bit, they expanded their empire until it extended from Paraguay to São Paulo and Bolivia; and they calculated well and annexed the Amazonian basin. In 1599, Father Juan Font made an expedition into the hills that form the headwaters of the Amazon in Peru, into the Campa territory; he presented a plan for the colonization of this area, which he described as "full of people and wonderful things"; but this plan was never translated into action, and "Soldiers of God" continued to cultivate the Amazonian basin. They have left us some interesting documents, such as the detailed map published in Quito in 1707 by Father Fritz, a German Jesuit, who spent thirty-seven years among the forest people. This map guided the La Condamine party a few years later.

BANDS OF EXPLORERS, BANDS OF SETTLERS

In northern Brazil, the missionary efforts of the Jesuits took them into the province of Maranon; the rule of the company was established there by an old preacher to the court of Lisbon, Father António Vieira, who in 1655 went on to obtain dominion—both spiritual and temporal—over the Amazon forest dwellers, who had never admitted the authority of the Church.

Two years later, the king of Portugal had outlawed descidas, the huge hunts designed to capture a quarry of slaves, and he would no longer authorize any expeditions that did not include a missionary, who was charged with "preaching religion and teaching agriculture." It became more and more difficult for the colonists to obtain manpower; the price of blacks was too high in Maranon, and the Jesuits only lent out their Indians six months of the year, demanding an under-the-table payment for them that was not altogether Christian....

Soon, the government was worried about the territorial ambitions of the Society and quietly started supporting *entradas* to take the Jesuits' territory away from them. The most active of these groups of raiders was based in São Paulo and commanded by Antonio Raposo Tavares, but all the raiding parties followed the same plan: descend on a village held by the Jesuits, attack—preferably by surprise—and clear it out, scattering the masters in cassocks and, of course, seizing their subjects. In this way, the Jesuits were driven back toward Paraguay, toward the Gran Chaco, and Brazil was able to secure its western and southern borders.

In the northern part of the country, it was not so easy to establish sovereignty. French buccaneers had managed to establish a colony there that had to be dislodged. The conflict with the Dutch was not resolved for years; in 1661, however, they agreed to withdraw. But Brazil had other border problems with the neighboring Spanish countries. The Tordesillas line, established by a papal bull of 1493, gave all the land west of Belem to Spain. A governor of the state of Para-Maranon, Jacob Raimundo de Noronha, secretly assembled a group of explorers, assigning Pedro Texeira as its leader. The troop that set out on 28 October 1637 was a veritable armada: seventy Portuguese, twelve hundred Indian warriors, along with slaves and women, the whole totaling more than two thousand people, aboard sixty-seven flatboats, which also held their food and weapons. They lasted an entire year, fighting the currents, constantly getting off course and struggling to find their way back without a guide, and maintaining a close watch on the Indians, whose defections kept multiplying. Their route was marked by the hamlets they settled, using them as bases for their activities. That is how Manaos was founded: Pedro Texeira established the outpost on a little hill overlooking the Amazon. By the end of 1638, after having made their way up the Rio Negro, and then the Napo, finishing their journey on foot, they made their entrance into Quito. No fools, the Spanish gave them a cool reception and sent Pedro Texeira back to Belem between two Jesuits; this did not prevent him from stopping at the mouth of the Japura River, on 16 August 1639, and solemnly taking possession of all the territory below it— *"terras, rios, navegaçoes, e comercios"*—in the name of the Portuguese Crown.

The following year Portugal threw off the Spanish yoke and declared its independence. Portugal was hardly in a favorable position. The Portuguese had incurred heavy debts to the Dutch and had lost their monopoly on the route to the Indies. The Brazilian authorities were called upon to find new resources. This revived the dreams that had driven the first conquistadores, resuscitated the Indian legends, and sent the adventurous off on a valiant quest for Eldorado and the Emerald Mountain. São Paulo fell for this dream of fabulous treasure, embracing the challenge and becoming the base for increasingly ambitious expeditions.

The first Portuguese may not have found Eldorado, but visions of gold and glory drew them onward, and so they did establish settlements in the mother lode, and they did strike it rich. The planters of northeastern Brazil grew wealthy in their little fiefdoms, with their slaves and their fields of sugarcane. The Paulista half-breeds on the roads through the *sertão* had a more glorious fate. For more than a century, they conducted furious crusades—which should not be confused with those of the honored bandits, the *cangaceiros*—spreading across the interior of the country. In their tireless vagabondage, a few supply centers acted as beacons; certain of these base camps put down roots, grew, and developed into market towns; their success was the other face of misfortune; but the bands of settlers whose impossible dream led them far from such ordinary preoccupations never knew a thing about it. *Auri sacra fames!*

Among the most famous feats: Antonio Raposo Tavares traveled more than eighteen thousand miles in four years conducting continuous raids. Setting out around the end of 1647, he first seized some Jesuits, sweeping through their territory to north of Asunción; always waging war, whether against Jesuits or Indians, the raiders went in search of the marvelous, sparkling metals and precious stones, finally traveling as far as Santa Cruz, then Sucre. By then famine, epidemics, and malaria had decimated his troops; of the two thousand or more who had set out, only fifty were left. Too few in number to brave the interior of the country, to face Indians and their ambushes, they decided to take advantage of the great rivers to carry them back to Belem. In spite of the quicksand that sometimes formed their only launch sites, in spite of the many rapids, they managed to navigate the Mamoré and the Madeira, and to travel down the Amazon to the Atlantic. They had extended the zone of Portuguese influence to the west, all the way from Belem to Potosi. One must salute these New World argonauts who gave their country its true dimensions.

Not too surprisingly, after Brazil became independent, these *bandeirantes,* or bands of explorers and settlers, became a national symbol. They were invoked when roads were cut, they were invoked when Brasilia was built. They are invoked when Indians are massacred. They are warrior heroes; apart from the search for gold and the murder of "redskins," their only concerns are subsistence and survival. (Significantly, *explorar,* "to explore," also means "to exploit" in Portuguese.)

Other nameless adventurers followed in the wake of the bandeirantes, seeking their fortune along the great rivers, crisscrossing the Amazon region in every direction. Whether they panned for gold or tapped rubber trees, all these men hated and feared the jungle; looking back at it, they saw no treasure, only terror.

But when it was entered humbly, without aggression, the forest revealed its secrets. It delighted naturalists. They were willing to endure anything, to withstand any hardship as they traveled about, marveling at the life they found. Arriving back in England, poorer than when he set out, his health shattered, young Henry Bates was a happy man: while in the Amazon he had discovered eight thousand new types of insects; his *Report on Insect Fauna in the Amazon Basin* is studded with enthusiastic descriptions of the jungle.

These naturalists, armed with their vials of cyanide, their butterfly nets, and their notebooks, are the explorers who started to unveil the Amazon, to demythologize it at least a bit. For these strange and stubborn men, these botanical dreamers, the jungle was laboratory and study, although rather dangerous ones, to be sure.

The Amazon has seen other equally inoffensive explorers pass through it; a few naïfs who did not believe in adventure, even more who believed in it too much. Here is one example.

THE ORDEAL OF MADAME GODIN

In 1770, the cry was heard as far as Paris: a tragedy, Madame Godin had died in the jungle. Madame Godin? In the jungle! What drama, what pathos; the facts were stranger than fiction.

The story began on 16 May 1735, in the port of La Rochelle, when Jean Godin set out for the equator with the expedition headed by Charles-Marie de la Condamine. His role in the project was fairly modest: it was his job to carry the instruments for the surveyors. Thanks to which, he had the time to seduce a beautiful Creole girl in the town of Riobamba. Isabela was thirteen years old, Godin was thirty: they were married.

When he had measured the meridian and completed his work, La Condamine went back to France via the Amazon, an itinerary that would be followed by Godin and his young wife. Jean Godin left Riobamba in 1749, alone. He was on a reconnaissance trip, traveling along the coast in search of a good ship, planning to hire it and sail back to pick up his family. "Everyone but you, sir," he wrote to La Condamine from Cayenne, "would be amazed that I am making one journey to fifteen hundred places with no other objective than to prepare for a second journey, but you would understand that in South America a man is more ready to travel about than in Europe." And he asked La Condamine to intervene with the Portuguese authorities, to help him hire a half-galley.

And time went by, in a monotone, with no seasons to mark its passage. In Riobamba, his four children had died, while Doña Isabela continued to wait for her husband. In Cayenne, Jean Godin continued to wait for his galley. And the galley finally arrived—*sixteen years later*—in 1765. Godin, who was suffering from a persecution complex, refused to board the ship; instead he sent a man he trusted, Tristan d'Oreasaval.

Eight months later, the galley anchored in the port of Iquitos, and Tristan waited at the mission of Las Lagunas for the arrival of Madame Godin. But the letters he sent to Quito and Riobamba never got out of the jungle. Instead, they traveled from mission to mission, giving rise to many a dinner conversation. So the news, carried by word of mouth, finally reached its destination, and Doña Isabela learned that her husband was alive, that he had sent a boat to search for her, that he was waiting for her arrival.

Her husband returned from the dead! Years of separation forgotten, Madame Godin set out to meet him, without a thought for the length of the trip. Her brothers, her servants, Joaquím, her faithful black manservant, and some Quechua slaves formed her unusual escort....

A week later, they arrived in Canelos, frozen and filthy, but relieved to have completed what they thought was the most difficult part of the journey. Alas! No more gardens, no more houses, no more mission; the entire settlement had been razed, burnt to the ground: smallpox had gotten there before them. One raft and one canoe, that is all they were able to dig out of the ruins. Doña Isabela went on with as many of her party and provisions as possible. They had to reach the galley, at all costs.

The next day almost cost them their all; one error in judgment and their raft was gone, swept away. The faithful Joaquím went off in the canoe to look for help.

A month later, Madame Godin, her companions, and her servants were still waiting. Finally the group launched another raft, with all their remaining equipment piled onto it. The craft lasted only long enough to crash into a tree trunk, which broke it in two. The entire group drowned. It had been too much of an ordeal. When Joaquím returned a few days later, he found no survivors.

Madame Godin was dead. The news spread. To Cayenne. To Riobamba. And to France, where it made the front pages of the newspapers. Several years later, *Magasin pittoresque* published a novelized version of the Godin story, because what began so badly turned out well and there was a happy ending: in 1770, a Portuguese galley entered the harbor at Cayenne; aboard it were Doña Isabela and her husband.

When the raft sank near Canelos, Madame Godin had been the only survivor. Two days later, she walked away from her seven dead companions and entered the jungle; with no way of knowing where she was, she traveled blindly, semiconscious. She stumbled along for days, keeping herself alive by eating "cinnamon apples" (cherimoyas) and palm leaves; after nine days of wandering, she was picked up by Shimagai Indians, who took her to the mission at Andoas. Weak and pale, she had only one thought: to get to Cayenne. "Having undertaken this trip in order to rejoin my husband, if I gave up, I would be guilty of thwarting the designs of providence." An Indian woman had offered her some clothing; the missionaries, a canoe. Madame Godin left to meet the galley that was still waiting for her. With her father and the faithful Joaquím, who had eventually caught up with her, she set out for Cayenne. After twenty years of separation, Jean Godin was reunited with his wife, who had been barely twenty years old when he left her.

A heroine in spite of herself, Madame Godin had escaped "the evil spell of the forest." The Amazon, for once, had been merciful.

DEATH IN THE AMAZON

With its shadows and its sepulchral peace, the Great Forest has continued to fascinate the *voyagistes,* the romantics among the explorers, including a few Robinsons in hiking shorts as well as the inevitable crashing bores of adventure. Dangerous adventures and aesthetic adventures. Scientific adventures. They share the same curiosity and the same mortal fear: the fear of death.

On 10 July 1950, along the path from Émerillons, a Guyanese policeman discovered the remains of an abandoned camp on the banks of the Tamouri River: a thatch of topinambour leaves and branches, a hammock suspended below it, a slightly damaged .22 long rifle, Passport No. 670 issued by the prefecture at Var, some blades ("Gillette") for an automatic razor, a packet of fishhooks, a pair of glasses.... Remnants of an impossible dream. Raymond Maufrais, young hero of the Resistance, had come to die of hunger and dysentery in a malign forest.

"Exploration, for me, is an adventure in purity and solitude," he had declared before setting out. He had come on a quest, in search of the feeling that he "truly existed, bearing his full responsibilities as a man and taking a risk that was (worth) the danger." And patterning his experience on certain initiation ceremonies, he believed that it was necessary to set about this venture by himself. But "living alone in the jungle requires knowledge," objected old Paul Lecointe. And Raymond Maufrais lacked that knowledge. So, the notebooks found in his camp trace a slow agony of exhaustion and starvation until his final collapse.

In the heart of the Mato Grosso, some twenty years before, Colonel Fawcett had written: "It is very cold at night and fresh in the morning; but toward the middle of the day, the heat and insects descend, and until ten o'clock at night we suffer a veritable martyrdom in camp.".... Fawcett and his son had never been seen again; they left a blond Indian boy, son of Jack Fawcett and an Indian woman. Defeat no longer threatens Maufrais. He has disappeared, never to be seen again.

Public opinion did not want to accept the death of Raymond Maufrais any more than it had accepted Fawcett's. It preferred to imagine an idyll among the blond Indians he had sought: crowned their king, he had become the white god of Tumuc-Humac. His father organized an expedition. His house filled with letters from all the people who wanted to accompany or simply to encourage him; crackpots and shady dealers, unscrupulous people eager to take advantage of the naïveté of a brave man, but also sentimental types willing to bet on the legend despite the odds.

"Papa Maufrais" undertook the torturous pilgrimage across the Amazonian wilderness. Chaos of leaves, giant plants. Profound desolation. At first he did not want to travel toward the Tamouri. Why should he, since the oracles do not believe his son is there. He went to the Tumuc-Humac mountains, legendary hiding place of the white Indians. This was the beginning of a confused quest, which took him from one end of the forest to the other, on the strength of the most extravagant tales, the most pitiful leads. Toward what new obsession? His skin was like parchment; his eyes, wild. What did he really want? Did he think that his sacrifice would make his son reappear?

Two Iliads for nothing. Two Odysseys in vain, with five columns on the front pages of the newspapers. He had carried his pain to indecent lengths. He was found in the Tamouri, very near Raymond's last camp; he was feverish, delirious, unable to speak.... Since then, in many other cases, the public has taken an ascetic point of view: admitting there is no hope does not stop one from continuing to expect a miracle.

Little by little, the Amazon region has yielded to exploration; since Bertrand Flornoy, the sources of the ocean-river seem less mysterious* and the Jivaro headhunters more human. Ethnographers and linguists methodically unravel its secrets. But adventurers, true to themselves, continue to stream down its great highways, to swindle those "shit-assed exotics," the Indians.

JUNGLE TRADERS

A sorry character soon appears on the scene, trailing along in the wake of the explorers, heading his canoe into the farthest reaches of the jungle. He is the jungle trader.

By 1865, the Reverend Father Antonio had drawn a portrait of these traders, concluding, "They are the *regatoes,* petty traders, whose canoes penetrate the most distant *sertoes* to do business with the Indians. It is hard to believe the frauds and injustices perpetrated by the vast majority of these men, taking advantage of the weakness or ignorance of their unfortunate clients. They sell them the shabbiest products at the most fabulous prices; obtaining the Indians' goods by force or trickery, always paying a terrible price, and often getting the heads of households drunk in order to dishonor their families more easily. In short, there is no immorality that is not practiced by these greedy adventurers."

The Portuguese were the first regatoes in the back country; then came the Jews, the Syrians, and the Turks. During the rubber boom, they swarmed to the four corners of the jungle interior. Missionaries, honest travelers, people angry at the mistreatment the Indians suffered, all denounced their breed. Peruvian writer Mario Vargas Llosa made one into a damned soul in his novel *The Green House.* But trading is still the favorite activity of whites in the Amazon, the only one they have pursued faithfully throughout this period. An archaic punishment? Their fundamental capitalism condemns them to wander the earth.

---

* In 1914, Bertrand Flornoy fixed them in the Huayhuash Cordillera, at an elevation of around sixteen thousand feet.

CITIES OF THE AMAZON

The Western builder of cities hesitates at the edge of Amazonia. It is easy enough to transpose the cities of southern Europe to the South American coasts or the Andean plateaus: a square plaza flanked by public buildings, religious or political; a residential section arranged like a checkerboard; there, the framework of a city.

In the forest, the white man is on shakier ground. Nonetheless, some villages were founded by the first conquerors. It was a solemn act of appropriation, a highly symbolic demonstration in the face of a menacing Cyclopean landscape. In planting the cross and the flag, Western man placed his mark on a small patch of land and integrated it into his system. But since fortune did not smile on him, why would he wish to linger in this filthy hole? And, besides, who came to the Amazon with the idea of remaining there? Take Barcelos, for example; what happened to this old capital of the Rio Negro, established by a Portuguese minister in 1780? Vianna Moog paints a desolate picture: "By the time it was visited by the naturalist Alexandre Rodriguez Ferreira, it had already been reduced to a repulsive sprawl of dilapidated houses. The ancient and imposing palace of Demarcaçoes, with its native roof of thatch and palm straw, was a glaring example of its ridiculous and grotesque architecture; the celebrated cloth factory had disappeared, as had the Carmelite convent and country house of the governor. And Borba, and Humaïta, and an infinity of little Amazonian villages that dared to call themselves cities."

It was a Portuguese law that had hampered any efforts to establish permanent settlements, however pathetic: until independence, Brazil was not allowed to develop its own industries. With only a few rare exceptions, the motherland had exclusive rights to manufacture products; the role of the colony was to supply raw materials. The urbanization of Brazil coincided with cycles of prosperity; first, sugar money, then coffee, then gold.... As each wave ebbed, it left a flotsam of abandoned cities, like skins shed by a snake.

Deep in Amazonia, the rubber boom revived hamlets that had been asleep for years and years. Manaos became the white city, the goal of all those who lived and died with the fever for black gold. When their dreams came true, the newly rich tried to make Manaos into their image of utopia. The area was surveyed. A real city was built, with plazas, gardens, paved streets, like Rio. Then it was settled, developed. It got bridges, a sewer system, electricity, telephones. And the first tramway in the Americas toiled over ten miles of tracks. And the floating docks of its port received steamers from Liverpool and Anvers. Nothing was too good for Manaos. Stone and rock were brought from the coast so it could be built "to last." Italian marble was imported for the palaces. The customs building was constructed in England and shipped to Manaos. And the Opera House! Seating fourteen hundred, it was made of a white marble streaked with red and had a cupola topped with polychrome tiles.... A new order had been launched. Money had taken the helm.

The illusion did not last. Today, in a city that has fallen back into lethargy, one hundred and eight thousand inhabitants are waiting.... Do they even know for what? The rush for rubber left them with nothing but a scorn for agricultural work, a taste for gambling, all-or-nothing, and perhaps a faint hope for a new monetary explosion. The avenues recite the litany of the petty trades that flourish in cities with few jobs: shoeshine boys, ice cream vendors, lottery ticket sellers, fourteen-year-old *filles sans joie*.... In the suburbs, it is the crowding together of hovels, reed huts on pilework, houseboats floating on brackish waters. But let the tourists come! They will find things to buy: polyglot parrots, polychrome crows, boas, mysterious balms, and all the "typical" trinkets of the jungle. And there are brand-new hotels so the tourists' Western complexions will not have to suffer; before 1970, the Tropical Manaos hotel offered them ready-made tropics: right in the jungle, or nearly, in a gigantic bubble, nearly nine hundred and eighty-five feet in diameter and four hundred and ninety-two feet high, all steel and glass, there is a hotel, a swimming pool, and an eight-hundred seat theater, several restaurants, a nightclub, an aquarium where guests can walk through a Plexiglas tube under the water, gardens, birds, flowers.... Never more than seventy-four degrees Fahrenheit and fifty percent humidity.... Climatized, sterilized, sanitized, the green hell has been humanized.

Iquitos, in the Peruvian Amazon, also grew into prosperity during the rubber boom. It still has a charming central plaza, two houses designed by Eiffel, a promenade alongside palaces whose frame tilework cannot conceal their decrepitude, palaces threatened by the river each time it rises; it also has the reputation of being a paradise for carousers, an image that puts a wicked gleam in the eyes of Lima residents.... Iquitos is in the same district as Belem, the floating ghetto of Indians and half-breeds, beloved of tourists who paddle around it because of its wealth of "local dolor." The Third World in 35 mm. Meat and dried fish; washerwomen, half-Indian and half-naked (because they wash their only dresses); sunbathers on the Amazon. There is also the sweet acrid odor of exotic fruit rotting. And if a man does not have the look of a guide, he can string up a little hammock with the guy who sells tobacco and local drugs and there drink *chuchuhuasi,* alcohol made from chopped bark, which is said to cure everything; they even think it is an aphrodisiac. Corrosive rotgut.

Is this all that "civilization" has been able to bring here? These triangles of filth and misery, this travesty of a house made from tin cans and planks, this bad alcohol to help them forget, to help them endure it. Here lies the Peruvian Amazon.

Chased from their Amazonian domain, attracted to the cities by the false hope of earning a living there, the Indians become rabble. The helots of the white caste system.

Brazilians as well as Peruvians, the people who live in the Amazonian districts often complain to their government about the penury in which they have been left; the slogan "an Amazonian Amazon" is more than just a clever phrase. In a strange response to their just demands, the Amazon basin has recently been declared a free zone. No restrictions on imports and no duty charged.

Manaos and Iquitos, which have become centers of illegal trade, are showing some signs of renewed activity; and even the little Peruvian town of Pucallpa—whose name means "red earth" in Quechua—on the Ucayali River has found a reason for being. Pitiful market town with no ships arriving to bring its port to life, it was suddenly swelled by every sort of store, mart, and emporium where the marvels of Western and Japanese industry could be piled high and sold. The whole village is on two streets: shops, vile hotels, shabby and stuffy theaters, bar-restaurants.... Merchants and traders, American evangelists (a family patriarch and a towheaded brood), colonels with a minimum of training, and, next to them, authentic Shipibo Indian maidens, beauties looking stunned and cautious.... On the banks of the river, black pigs and vultures take care of the municipal hygiene and eat the garbage.... But where is Pucallpa's hospital? Why these power failures? Why no safe water? No sewers? Blame it on the people who have stayed in Pucallpa but have not thought about it. They are used to living with false fronts, and amassing fortunes that they plan to spend somewhere else. Far from the tropics.

Is the forest about to be plunged into a new cycle? On 3 March 1955, oil started flowing at Nova Olinda, twelve hours by boat from Manaos, on the Madeira River. In Peru, the International Petroleum Company is exploring the region of Madre de Dios, prospectors with a deadly passion. And the business of exploitation goes on....

BRASILIA, A CONCRETE GALATEA

In Brazil, the hope of taming the Amazon has been growing stronger. Brasilia is one manifestation of this dream. "After having camped for centuries on the edge of the ocean, Brazil is finally taking possession of its territory," declared President Kubitschek one day. Brasilia provides a symbol of Brazil's future, an era when the west will finally be conquered, besides serving as proof that Brazil is an adult country.... There has never been a city more charged with significance.

Brasilia is located in the geographical center of Brazil. In 1883, dom Jean Bosco had a vision of the future capital: "One night I had a dream in which I found myself transported by angels to a grand railroad station full of people. I boarded a train that traveled through Amazonian forests, crossed torrential rivers, and climbed the peaks of the Cordillera. Soon the train arrived in an Indian village where I witnessed the martyrdom of Pedro Sacilloti and João Fuchs, the pair of missionaries hacked to death with machetes. Then I traveled on, soon arriving at the foot of the mountains. Suddenly, the earth opened in front of me, and I saw the fabulous mass of riches hidden there. A few courageous men were risking incredible danger attempting to wrest these inestimable treasures from the ground. A divine voice spoke: 'When the wealth hidden within these mountains is mined, this place will see the dawn of a great civilization, a Promised Land, which will flow with more than milk and honey. Then prosperity such as has never been seen before will prevail....'"

Seen from the air, Brasilia looks like a beautiful bird with its wings outstretched on the red laterite of the Mato Grosso. A white bird. "The shape of Brasilia grows out of the basic gesture to mark and lay claim to a site: two lines intersecting each other at right angles, nothing other than the sign of the cross." This double articulation connects the blocks of buildings by the city planner Lucio Costa and the architect Oscar Niemeyer. The official buildings are aligned along the "monumental" axis; the curving transverse has residential buildings constructed on pilings, the "supercuadra": eleven blocks of six-story buildings and thirty-three blocks of three-story build-ings, each about seven hundred and ninety feet on a side, large enough to house three thousand people. In less than four years, a futuristic vision has been splashed over the landscape. In the process, sixty billion cruzeiros have gone down the drain (one dollar was worth one hundred and thirty cruzeiros when Kubitschek began his term in 1956, one hundred and ninety when his term ended in 1961, and fourteen hundred and fifty three years later). Disregard of economic priorities, crippling gigantism. Above all, this bloodless "concrete Galatea," with no back country to support it, is a master-piece of waste.

"*Não, não vou para Brasilia,*" sang the masked revelers at the carnival in Rio in 1959. Officials, high and low alike, responded with a sour face: they were forced by law to settle in the young capital. And before long "Cidade Libre"—the plank huts that had housed the equipment of the stonemasons—and what was pompously labeled "Nucleo Bandeirante" saw the influx of the starving people of the northeast, a population without hope and with-out initiative. Soon, Cidade Libre was not enough: the plateau became infested with shantytowns, gradually swelling and rooting more firmly. The "Turks" had a monopoly on small business in the shantytowns. These out-lying satellite towns grew up with the consent and under the direction of Novocap, the developer, and without the knowledge of Costa and Niemeyer. The euphoria of the first years evaporated.

But isn't this westward expansion really only the erection of new *favelas* on the edge of a city so grand that a person must own a car in order to move through it? "In Brasilia," stated Pierre Monbeig, the geographer, "I felt like I was in the stratosphere; I do not know if the stratosphere is a very com-fortable or practical place for a capital city."

Awaiting the judgments of history, we must ask a few questions: Brasilia may be a monument to the spirit, but whose spirit is captured there? Do mestizo Indian Brazilians really need an Athens? Yes, Brasilia fills us with fear: the West became humanistic and triumphed, but how long will this last?

With the construction of this fantastic project, the Mato Grosso region was thrown into a frenzy. The unusual situation presented a rare opportu-nity; hoping to profit from the delirious mood, speculators swarmed to the area in search of land, in search of cocoa, in search of rubber. And in the name of order and progress, Indians were sacrificed without the slightest pang of regret. Brazil is loyal to all of its excesses.

From Orellana to Brasilia: four and a half centuries of efforts to invent and destroy the Amazon. The pioneers scratched its surface but never really knew it. Even technological civilization has not yet been able to touch it—and this, in spite of Brasilia—at least the vast majority of it.

However, according to a study done by UNESCO, the Amazon basin is capable of feeding a billion people. This assertion has reawakened Brazil's dream of El Dorado. Experts ponder, plan, theorize; journalists speculate on it, politicians live off it. Some resources have already been found: iron, manganese, oil. The gringos are planning to construct a dam on the Rio Negro. In the West, propaganda—and bulldozers—are nibbling away at the rain forest pie....

What will be the outcome of this dubious contest? Amazonia sends out its voracious tentacles and swallows up the most audacious projects. Statistics are equally cruel: the jungle zone contains no more than a fraction of a man per square mile.

THE QUEST FOR
RUBBER AND
ITS HEROES

T HE RUSH FOR
BLACK GOLD

THE QUEST FOR RUBBER FORMS
a dramatic chapter in the Amazonian saga, the story of dozens of incredible
fortunes, of hundreds of successes and thousands of deaths. It is an instruc-
tive story. The rubber boom provided the most potent image of success in
the period around 1910: a rubber baron lighting a cigar with a hundred mil-
reis bill in the Opera House in Manaos.

That was during its heyday, when the whole world applauded rubber's
magic act, the way it could imitate leather, turn into a ball and bounce,
change its shape, and make the marks on paper disappear.... But its debut
was more humble. It got its first break from two French eggheads, La Condamine and François Fresneau; the former introduced it this way: "It can be
made into unbreakable containers, into boxes, into hollow bowls that can be
flattened by pressing on them, but spring back into their initial shape when
released." The Maina Indians call it *cahuchu* (from *ca,* "wood," and *uchu,* "to
trickle" or "to weep"). It was under this name that it made its entry to the
Academy of Sciences in 1745. This first appearance drew good notices, but
it was not until Charles MacIntosh began to work with it that it was seen as
anything more than an eraser. Long after the Mexicans or the Aztecs had
formed it into balls to use in their ballgames, it was forced to endure the fog
and rain of London; unfortunately, it could not stand the climate: in the heat,
it melted; in the cold, it cracked; in either case, it stank. As a *mackintosh* it

was only a partial success. However, it did have its admirers; Charles Nelson Goodyear wrote about it: "There is probably no other inert substance whose qualities so provoke curiosity, astonishment, and admiration in the minds of men." And so he proceeded to vulcanize it. Treated with sulfur, it became more flexible, less difficult, and much more attractive. It was soon called upon to play new roles, and with the horseless carriage it finally found itself firmly established.

It became the toast of Manaos. It was able to buy everything, except morality: the new millionaires behaved like soldiers on a spree; camp followers did a roaring trade; diamonds rolled across green gametables; the fifty-dollar champagne flowed. Brothels were packed. Crime multiplied: illegal gambling, theft, and scandal. The ruling code: violation, transgression, consumption. Here, we can paraphrase Balzac: there is only one material good with a value so absolute that man feels he must seek it. That good ... is black gold. Black gold represented every force that drives humanity.

THE RUBBER TAPPER

Far from this tumult, rubber tappers procured the black gold. A hut up on pilings, preferably atop a hill, to escape the floods of the rainy season; a network of narrow trails, the *estradas,* which twist and knot between the giant trees. That is the realm of the rubber tapper, his absurd prison without walls. Tirelessly, he travels the same paths, like a blind mule working the pump in a well.

Rising before dawn, he starts his rounds, equipped with a knife, his *faca,* and a lamp, the *coronga,* that he wears on his head like a coal miner. On his first circuit of the estradas, he cuts into the hevea trees to make the latex flow. After a morning's work, he stops for a lonely lunch; it is always the same: manioc mush, a little dried meat or canned tunafish. In the afternoon, he visits the trees again, to gather the latex that has dripped into the zinc buckets hanging below the "feather" or "fishbone" cuts. Returning to his hut around five o'clock, the man still has to shape the ball of rubber; over a fire of uripiri nuts or fresh kindling, he slowly turns the stick on which the rubber embryo grows each day as new layers of latex harden in the smoke. After a few weeks, this *bolacha* will have reached the size his boss demands, weighing anywhere between sixty-five and one hundred and fifty pounds. He must then carry it to the edge of the river or to the foreman's depot.

Like a miner, condemned to the eternal shadow of the forest, to the dampness of his cave, he does not even enjoy the comfort of companionship: no comrade with whom to share his *mala suerte,* hard luck and trouble; his only communication is with the hundred and fifty or two hundred hevea trees scattered about his patch of suffering. He has no real progeny, just the blackish ball that swells slowly; too slowly most of the time, since the boss demands an average of two and one-half gallons of latex a day and "the whip exacts its fee, sparing no one." Every moment is devoted to this vital project. The boss, after all, doesn't he provide for everything? Everything a man could want is available at the foreman's store; and it is all free; that is where the rubber tapper was taken as soon as he arrived; he found tools, provisions, kerosene, liquor, and a blank page under his name on the storekeeper's register: the page soon filled up. He had no chance of leaving, ever; a captive of credit, he was working just to make his payments; lured into a trap, with everything arranged so that the list of his debts grew longer on each of his trips: merchandise at fabulous prices, balance falsified so it is always greater than his production. From then on, there is an additional stimulus: fear. If his harvest is too small, the whip. The whip again if his boss is not happy, and if he cannot imagine any more refined tortures.

Malnourished, wracked by fevers, the rubber tapper does not have much hope of escape. If, by chance, the foremen do not catch him and beat him like a beast, he will rot in the underbrush, defeated by hunger, exhaustion, and folly.

BASIC CAPITALISM

Between this pitiful creature and the powerful international rubber magnate, there is a chain of intermediaries who keep the system running smoothly. There are the cruel foremen who oversee a work force mortally weakened by hunger. These mercenaries are half-breeds or Indians brought from Barbados. The foreman's job is to make the workers respect the law of the rubber plantation; and woe to any foreman who is not willing to wield the whip—he will soon be added to the list of those found dead in the jungle. His compensation: an occasional spree in the nearest village; bad cane liquor and pitiful prostitutes, Indian women taken from their tribes.

At the head of the troupe, the boss. Absolute master of the rubber plantation, his power scarcely extends beyond it. Local *caudillo,* satrap of the watershed, his cruelty gives him the illusion of a power that he does not possess. Because he is at the mercy of a "a trading cartel" that distributes merchandise and also provides supplies and materials; he is powerless against this intermediary group; it is free to buy and sell at whatever price it chooses since it has a monopoly on transportation throughout the region; without this group, he suffocates. Unable to combat its tyranny, he is forced to bend to it and increase his production; this demand is passed along to the rubber tappers.

The best guarantee of the efficiency of this system: the rivalries that set the men against one another. The rubber tappers will murder one another for a few extra quarts of latex. The foremen are pitiless in their denunciations of anyone who tries to withhold any part of the crop from the *establecimiento*. The bosses carry on an endless war among themselves, for slaves, for money, for new areas to exploit. In the rubber empire, "the only law is the Winchester"; the plunder of the Amazon, the devastation of its cultures, is the system's order.

Civilized man, while not without daring, is the paladin of destruction. "There was a magnificent courage during the age of these pirates, who made their peons into slaves, exploited the Indians, struggled against the jungle.... Delirious with malaria, they shed their consciences and went armed with only a Winchester and a machete, and they were willing to take any risk and undergo the most hideous torments, dreaming of wealth and pleasures under the rigors of the harshest weather, always starved, often nearly naked, since their clothes rotted on their bodies. Finally, one day, on a rock on a riverbank, they threw up a hut and started calling themselves 'captains of industry.' As the forest was their enemy, they did not know who to fight so they threw themselves upon one another and killed and enslaved one another during the intervals between their war with the people of the forest. And the paths they have cut through these countries look like an invasion of termites: the *caucheros* ... destroy millions of trees each year."

THE RUBBER BARONS

"But only the most foolish plunge into the forest," notes Ferreira de Castro, adding that, "Fiends, schemers, dealers settle in Belem and Manaos to make money, to obtain the maximum profit from the misery and suffering of those men who risk their lives to extract the gum."

Julio Cesar Arana, a small hatmaker in the village of Rioja at the foot of the Peruvian Andes, was a clever businessman. He roamed the entire western Amazon selling his hats; he followed the routes of the rubber convoys, and everywhere he went, he heard the tales of fortunes earned quickly, honestly or not, and of the beautiful city of Manaos, which had become the capital of the black gold. A first store, opened in 1888 at Tarapoto on the Huallaga, could not satisfy his appetite for wealth. Arana was ambitious; it did not take him long to tire of scouring the region to make a 400 percent profit on the gewgaws and gear that he traded in production centers. In 1890, he announced to his brother-in-law that the time had come to move on to serious business—he was going to make a trip to northeast Brazil, to the Ceara, where a famine was raging. He brought back twenty men who would work for nothing, each with a "labor contract" that condemned him forever, with no hope of remission; on the first day, when he charged them seventy pounds for food and a few paltry tools that were worth a quarter of that, his infernal machine was set in motion. In 1896, Arana settled his family in Iquitos; the empire of J.C. Arana Brothers was founded.

Following the discoveries of MacIntosh and Goodyear, the demand for rubber grew. In 1895, a race between Bordeaux and Paris demonstrated the superiority of the pneumatic tire, invented by the Michelin brothers. Arana increased his contracts with Lisbon, Paris, and especially London. By 1907, he was one of the great rubber barons; he had set up his offices in Manaos and sent his family to Europe. The same year, the ordinances of the Peruvian Amazon Rubber Company were registered in London: capital, one million pounds sterling; director, Julio Cesar Arana. Between 1910 and 1911, the Putumayo region, in which he held exclusive rights, supplied his company with four thousand tons of rubber, at the cost of some thirty thousand human lives. Brazilian exports went from thirty tons in 1825 to twenty-six thousand seven hundred and fifty in 1900 and to forty-two thousand in 1910. With a rare energy and tenacity, and a complete lack of scruples, Arana managed to take the lion's share. A vast territory, thousands of slaves, patrols of armed guards, a transportation network; from Rioja to Manaos, he had reached his goal: dealing as an equal with the lords of black gold.

The most powerful of them all, a Bolivian, was Don Nicolas Suarez: he was extremely rich, extremely greedy, and entirely lacking in humor. He is the very model of the colonizer. In 1872, in the Beni region, he founded one of the first companies for the exploitation of rubber. He was twenty-one years old at the time. Searching for new rubber zones, the six Suarez brothers—of whom Nicolas was the youngest—decided to begin prospecting in the northern part of the country, to the horror of the Indians whose domain it had been for centuries. (Misery and disease, the chaos of trees and water, the jungle's immensity, paradoxically, these were the only defense of the Indians, whose fighting techniques may have been picturesque but were not much of a match for firearms and germ warfare.) In 1873, the Indians began to resist the Creole invasion: Gregorio Suarez paid for their anger with his life. His men were crossing the Madeira River and he found himself alone on the beach; some Caripuna "Indian braves" captured him and cut off his head. Was it an act of vengeance? Hadn't the Suarez brothers left bottles of poisoned liquor on the beaches in order to exterminate the Indians and seize their lands? Whatever the case, Nicolas Suarez was determined to avenge his brother. He arrived a few days later to lead a genocidal campaign against the Caripuna. He was relentless, pitiless: when his campaign ended, there was not a single Caripuna survivor.

In 1882, he made Cachuela Esparanza the center of his commercial enterprises: with a railroad link to Decauville, which passed over a section of the Beni River that was impossible to navigate, he was able to earn substantial profits; with a naval yard, where steamships and motor launches could dock, he was able to ensure the distribution of the *bolachas*. In 1893, a company was formed, Société Suarez Frères.

Upon the death of his brothers, Nicolas Suarez found himself in possession of a veritable empire: nearly fifteen million acres of land (more than Belgium and Holland combined), two hundred thousand head of cattle, and an annual production of two thousand tons of rubber. He employed seven thousand men.

But there was a dark cloud hanging over this picture: in northern Bolivia, the area around Acre had become the scene of fighting and guerrilla activity; Brazilian and Bolivian rubber tappers were contesting the ownership of the hevea trees. Having proclaimed its independence in 1902, the young republic of Acre declared war on Nicolas Suarez, principal occupant of the contested area. This led to a "Texas-style" war of secession. Nicolas Suarez invoked Law 44—that of the Winchester and surprise attacks—and raised his own army, which he called "Colonne Porvenir" for the village where it trained. The war lasted seven years. In the end, Bolivia gained the advantage in the struggle, but the conflict was settled only after difficult arbitration by Argentina. According to the treaty at Petropolis, the land around Acre was given to Brazil, and an indemnity of fifty million francs, as well as a number of other compensations, were awarded to Bolivia; among the most important concessions, Brazil was required to construct the Madeira-Mamoré railroad, which would give Bolivia access to the Atlantic.

The centers of rubber production had been unable to operate throughout the period of hostilities, but the Suarez fortunes were salvaged by the boom of 1910. When the collapse occurred, Don Nicolas Suarez was lucky: he managed to shift his enterprise to the exploitation of Para nuts. But after his death in 1940, his forty children, legitimate and illegitimate, ran the business into the ground, and the inheritance was frittered away.

The agrarian reform that followed the revolution of Paz Estenssoro, which redistributed the land to the peasants, dealt a death blow to the business.

Go to Cachuela Esperanza today, and you will see the Pando Theater—crumbling for the last twenty years—and a tiny chapel where Mass is no longer heard, and two 1930s cars, abandoned to the erotic play of lizards....

A FIRST TASTE OF DISAPPOINTMENT

In the euphoria of its early years, Manaos wore the mask of a perpetual carnival, with the "barons" reigning over the parade of rubber onto international markets. No one paid any heed to the wild rumor of rubber plantations in Malaysia. In Malaysia? But it was this thrust of fate that ended an incredible swashbuckling adventure, dealing a death blow to Manaos's drunken celebration. It all started in 1870. British industry was using more and more rubber; the Amazonian jungle was being destroyed; the rubber monopoly was making outrageous demands. It was necessary to find a British solution. And since the most productive rubber trees were in Brazil, England acquired Brazilian stock ... in spite of protectionist laws forbidding the export of seeds and plants. At first there was failure; the seeds did not survive this exile. But, in 1876, an English agent, Henry Alexander Wickham, departed Brazil on board the freighter *Amazonas* carrying no fewer than seventy thousand seeds collected along the banks of the Tapajos River; the customs officer at Belem had seen nothing. A few weeks later, after painstaking cultivation by the botanists of Kew Garden, the precious plants were shipped to Ceylon, Singapore, and Java. Carefully planted, carefully tended, these trees had a yield three and four times greater than that of the wild rubber trees of Amazonia. A docile work force ensured rational exploitation of the product; each coolie could care for an average of four hundred trees a day, each rubber tapper, one hundred and fifty. Amazonian supremacy had been challenged.

When eighty-two hundred tons of Asian rubber were thrown onto the market in 1910, Amazonian producers began to bend to the competition; the pound of rubber that was worth five shillings three in 1907 now was worth only four shillings eight. By 1914, the party was over: Asia controlled the market with a production of seventy-one thousand tons, while Brazil produced only thirty-seven thousand; the price of rubber fell to two shillings nine. In Manaos, the curtain went down on the spectacle. The extras deserted the scene: its extravagance had become impossible. Thirty years of stories had become history.

FORD IN THE AMAZON

But the Amazon exerts such a strong power of attraction that one expects disaster to be followed by a miracle. And that is what happened!

To escape the control of his British suppliers, Henry Ford decided to plant hevea trees in the Amazon. It was a simple problem: the land was still wild; domesticate it and increase its productivity—a simple matter of order and progress! He set to work in an area as large as a North American state. First order of business: provide for the welfare of the workers. The entire jungle city was assembled in Dearborn, Michigan, and then this capital of Fordlandia was taken apart and the pieces shipped on boats that carried it to far-off Tapajos.

There, the bulldozers destroyed the forest; knocking over trees, razing the land, and erecting the buildings sent from Dearborn. The project had everything: apartments for the workers, villas for the managers, a cafeteria, hospital, drugstore. In the whole history of the rubber industry, there had never been anything like it!

The jungle surrounding this center disappeared, replaced by a plantation larger than all those of Malaysia rolled into one. Two years was all it took for the American's trees to start producing and for the world rubber market to collapse. Was it divine justice?

In 1936, an article by Edward Tomlinson in the *Colliers* of 12 December boasted, "In the very heart of a region where archeologists and scholars possessed by the demon of adventure have gone to search for mythic cities and tribes descended from Phoenician traders, or other ancient peoples who might be wandering in the jungle, Henry Ford is laying the foundation for a grand civilization."

But that was not the last word. Henry Ford's policy of paying high wages led to a disaster, as the Brazilian landowners, the "colonels," paid five cruzeiros per day to their workers, and Ford paid between forty and one hundred. Which meant that in a few days a man could earn enough to live for a month. Why work any longer? Half-time workers became the norm in Fordlandia. This made perfect sense, at least to the *caboclos;* apparently Henry Ford did not find his own work ethic in this new land, any more than he would find his money. And then, too, these brave men did not seem to savor the three ready-cooked meals he supplied them; these underfed provincials preferred their pots of beans and their detestable dried meat to the healthy nourishment, well-balanced and wholesome, that they were served; the way they had of tearing apart the cafeteria and bellowing "Down with spinach!" struck fear into the whole countryside.

And that was not all! Problems began to multiply. A shortage of laborers, union agitation, surprising technical difficulties, unforeseen and unforseeable: the hevea trees needed the green shade of the forest, they wilted in the sun. Those that survived developed "leaf disease"; the epidemic ran along the beautiful straight rows of the plantation, there were no obstacles to the spread of the spores! A decision was made: bring in new plants … from the Far East. But, oh the thankless trees, these Brazilo-Malaysian heveas refused to readapt to their native country! For Henry Ford, his spinach, and his bulldozers, it meant defeat.

After the attack on Pearl Harbor, it was necessary to compensate for the loss of Asiatic rubber: the plantations had trouble supplying a tenth of the rubber needed by the Ford Motor Company alone. There was a return to the traditional method of exploiting the forest; eighteen thousand rubber tappers were recruited from the coast and were forced to submit to this renewed exploitation. Then came the invention of synthetic rubber. In 1946, Ford abandoned the business; the Brazilian government bought back his model city for two hundred and fifty thousand dollars. His Amazonian dream had cost him fifteen million dollars.

THE MADEIRA-MAMORÉ RAILROAD

"Under every tie, there lies a body." This statement comes back to us as we read an announcement in the Brazilian newspapers in May 1966: the Madeira-Mamoré railroad is being retired from service. Behind this bankruptcy, Warrant No. 501 conceals a hideous face; the railroad cost thirty million dollars and several thousand lives during its construction alone. "This country," according to one entrepreneur, "is a slaughterhouse; men cannot survive in it. The route that is being laid passes through a wild jungle, where swamps and porphyry cliffs alternate. With all the capital in the world and half its workers, it would still be impossible to complete this railroad." And if the railroad was built, in spite of this dire prophecy, which ultimately proved false, one must acknowledge the daring nature of this huge gamble and the unusual character of the international group that was willing to undertake it. One chronicler of the era notes that on a single day the company hospital housed patients of twenty-five nationalities who were suffering from thirty-nine diseases. In the first year of construction, deaths occurred pell-mell, striking workers from every country: one Bolivian, nineteen Spaniards, thirty-five Brazilians, five Portuguese, and one Norwegian. In 1909, the death register showed four hundred and twenty-five deaths, the majority of them men from Sweden and the Antilles. . . .

Thus, to develop the shortest possible route to England, by building tracks along the course of the Madeira River (which is not navigable because of its rapids) in order to reach the Amazon and then the Atlantic, the rubber dynasty engaged 21,717 men to wage a war that had no victors. Forty-one years of this utopia. From 1871 to 1912, nearly two hundred and twenty-six miles of line were imposed on the jungle. The workers lived on bread, molasses, and whiskey, and death was no stranger to them. Dysentery, beriberi, yellow fever. "Not to mention the arrows the Caripuna Indians shoot at us, which fly dashedly fast," recalled Francisco Ferreira Brandão, survivor of the rail battle. One of those miraculously spared.

The Madeira-Mamoré railroad, christened the "Mad Mary" by American engineers, deserves to survive; it represents a splendid wager with nature, as well as a defiance of the most fundamental laws of profit and loss. It never earned back its cost. Here is a look at the epic of the Mad Mary.

JOURNAL OF THE MAD MARY

1861
Bolivian General Quentin Quevedo has issued a statement containing this surprising declaration: "We envisage the completion of a communication route on the banks of the Madeira River." At this time, the experts are not sure if a road or a canal is planned. "The Brazilian government has agreed

to study the project with us," General Quentin added, concluding with the opinion that "the Madeira-Mamoré junction will be of tremendous strategic importance." An official commission, composed of General Quentin and an engineer named Martin da Silva, has been set up to survey the river.

October 1867
On the tenth of this month, a pair of brothers, José and Francisco Keller, began a trip up the Madeira River by canoe. They have started marking the proposed route.

October 1868
The Keller brothers have given up. "The project, which we estimate will cost eight million five hundred thousand cruzeiros, will never be completed if the government does not increase its support," stated Francisco Keller.

20 April 1870
Emperor Don Pedro II granted the contract to the Madeira & Mamoré Railways Company and to its president, Colonel George Earl Church.

1 November 1871
Work has begun: two engineers and twenty-eight Indians have been sent to the site to strike the first machete blows. Teams of workers are expected any day.

Early 1872
The project is under way.

Late 1872
Insurmountable difficulties. The "construction project in the jungle" must be abandoned. Our correspondent in Rio de Janeiro reports that public works construction stocks have plummeted. A quote from the market: the value per share has fallen from sixty-eight to eighteen.

1876
Philadelphia newspapers report that the Collins brothers have set sail for Brazil. They plan to travel to the area above the Madeira rapids and open a new Eden to civilization.

Shipwreck of the Metropolis

The Collins brothers have lost five hundred tons of rails, two hundred tons of equipment, and eighty men. The survivors have decided to remain in North Carolina. Collins, after a stormy meeting, during which his backers demanded that he spell out his intentions, declared, "We have made a wager with nature and we have every intention of seeing it through!"

New Difficulties

Chaos reigns at the work camp of the Madeira-Mamoré railroad following the mutiny of Italian and Hindu workers demanding higher wages. They are expected to be replaced by American workers. The ringleaders have been arrested and sent home. Seventy-five Italians have deserted the camp and are presently trying to reach Bolivia to rally that country behind their cause. The climate, working and health conditions, together with national antagonisms, provide a partial explanation of the revolt. "It is simply unbelievable —in the course of four kilometers, we encountered six ravines more than thirty meters across," we were told by one of the men in charge of the project. In response to a question about possible sanctions against the fugitives, his only reply was: "One way or another, lost in the jungle, they will find the death they deserve."

Collins Workers Crack

E. Williams, project foreman, made this report: "Yesterday, at the end of the afternoon, one of my men opened fire on his comrades. He shouted at the top of his lungs: 'I have the devil on my tail! I have the devil on my tail!' We overpowered him and shut him in an outhouse. We have five hundred and fifty workers, and two hundred and sixty are sick right now," he explained.

A communiqué from the civil guard in Belem indicates that "three hundred of the Collins workers have fled to Belem." The municipal authorities are worried about their presence in this city, where the word *gringo* has become synonymous with *bum.*

Collins Bankruptcy

Reverses suffered in the past few months, and continuing labor problems, have forced Collins to declare bankruptcy. This news stunned the thousands connected to his company. His wife is reported to have suffered a nervous collapse.

17 November 1903
Bolivia and Brazil have signed a treaty at Petropolis. It cedes all territory north of the Abuna River and west of the Madeira to Brazil in exchange for the construction of a railroad between Madeira and Mamoré, linking San Antonio and Guajara-Mirin. This will give Bolivia access to the Atlantic.

Summer 1907
A telegram reaches us: "Workmen on site—work of clearing and cutting begins."

Early 1908
The firm of May, Jekyll, and Randolph have taken up the challenge: Robert H. May, Burt Jekyll, and "King John" Randolph, three entrepreneurs who specialize in railroad building have been hired by Sir Parcival Farquhar, who is planning to restart work on this huge project. Sir Parcival says only, "This should give a new vigor to the enterprise, because these men are *winners*."

Para, January 1908
The local newspaper contains the story of three hundred and fifty Spaniards from Cuba arriving in Brazil aboard the freighter *Amanda*. Only sixty-five passengers are willing to disembark; the majority of the passengers believe the rumors coming from Porto Velho, a city three thousand miles from Para, of fantastic epidemics raging through the entire Madeira-Mamoré region. The mutineers are afraid that the terms of their contract will not be respected.

Recruiting Problems Worsen
Germany, Spain, Portugal, and Italy are all boycotting the job offers of the company's recruiters. Tension is mounting on the job site. Six hundred German workers, brought from Baltic ports, took one look at Porto Velho and refused to disembark. Those who agreed to get off the ship rose in revolt after only a week, and six of them, having stolen some supplies and empty cement barrels, attempted to reach Manaos by raft.

The quinine scandal has lowered the morale of the workers, increasing the atmosphere of open rebellion. It seems that these capsules—which cost up to twenty pounds a piece—contain nothing but a mixture of lime and bicarbonate of soda!

The Line Will Pay
Having prepared the balance sheet for the year, Sir Parcival Farquhar's aide outlined the financial situation of the company, concluding that "the total budget of two million two hundred and fifty thousand pounds must be tripled." When asked whether the company can ever make a profit, he answered simply, but forcefully, "The line will pay!"

February 1908
Five headless bodies have washed up on a beach along the Madeira River. They have been identified as the remains of the German fugitives.

March 1908
Doctor Carl Lovelace and a team of fifteen interns have arrived from Panama. During the welcoming ceremony, the head of the mission made this statement: "We plan to build a modern hospital in Candelaria, two miles from here. We will be able to care for three hundred sick people in it." After describing its internal arrangement and sanitary measures, Doctor Lovelace expressed his commitment to enforcing them: "Prophylactic measures will be adopted willingly or they will be imposed!" A group of specialists has been hired to give a healthy push to the project.

After Doctor Lovelace, eight hundred Spaniards have arrived in the Amazon from the work camps on the Panama Canal. The Madeira-Mamoré Company had offered them twice the salary they were earning there.

April 1908
The North Americans celebrate Independence Day in Porto Velho—with a picnic and a baseball tournament.

November 1909
Thirty-one miles of line have been completed.

End of 1909
Eighteen hundred workers have been hired for the construction of a section extending fifty-four miles into the jungle, the next step in the project according to the engineers.

May 1910
Opening of the Jaci-Parana post, at mile fifty-six.

News in Brief

Warning to Drinkers. Two men, caught drinking water that had not been boiled, have been executed.

New Indian Drama. Five men working with earth-moving equipment were killed during a scuffle with some hostile Caripuna Indians. It seems likely that a dispute over a trade caused this incident. As a result, Sir Parcival, hoping to avoid future problems, officially prohibited any commerce with the Indians. Violators will be discharged without pay.

Cows versus Mules. As mules from Arkansas and Missouri perish in the heat, they are being replaced by cattle, which are better adapted to the tropical climate.

Reinforcements. Sixty-eight Greeks from the island of Crete have been hired.

The freighter *Capella* arrived, carrying twelve Baldwin locomotives, these are constructed of Pittsburgh steel and burn Swansea coal.

Cargo unloaded: oranges and pears from California, onions, bottled water, several head of cattle, quinine in twenty-five ton lots, and, from Australia, a load of eucalyptus railroad ties.

A Reminder. It is illegal to begin a meal without taking a quinine capsule. Company guards are watching!

Lay Off Liquor and Women. The San Antonio tavern has been declared off-limits. Scotch MacGregor and Arthur N. Clean, who unknowingly drank rubbing alcohol, have been off their feet for two months.

Two Dead. The cabinetmaker who built the company's coffins was found dead this morning, apparently infected by the corpses whose final resting places he constructed.

X was treated with potassium permanganate after being bitten by a *machacuy* snake. He succumbed a quarter of an hour later.

(Late October 1910: mile ninety-four.)

30 April 1912
Workers lay the final tie. Triumphant celebration of the inauguration of the line. It is nearly two hundred and twenty-six miles long, twenty-seven more than were anticipated.

1931
The Brazilian government has purchased the Madeira-Mamoré line, for less than one million dollars.

1956

On an official inspection tour, the governor of Rondonia has traveled the line's two hundred and twenty-six miles at a speed of five miles per hour. The rails are bent, the steam engines huff and puff. Still, the governor states that he is satisfied with the condition of the equipment.

Two weeks after the governor of Rondonia's visit, an engine derails because of a loose axle. It was pulling twenty-eight cars....

25 May 1966

Bill 501 orders the cancellation of Madeira-Mamoré service; officials promise a new route to replace it.

So ends our little diary of the death train. Under every tie lies a body. Actually, the catchphrase errs in its pessimism, since the Madeira-Mamoré railroad recorded 6,208 deaths in laying 549,000 ties. But let us not mix up men and railroad ties to concoct ridiculous equations—6,208 men died in vain to build the Mad Mary.

SO ENDS THE SAD TALE OF THE QUEST FOR RUBBER

Fortunes made and lost. Ghost towns and phantom railroads. Plundered forests. Deaths, more deaths than anyone could count. Atrocities, more atrocities than anyone could imagine. For money, always for money, at the behest of a handful of shareholders, the Great Forest was deliberately transformed into the property of tragedy. With the degrading servitude of the rubber tappers. With the systematic extermination of the Indians; we will not go into the details of this terrible disgrace now; we will return to it later, since it is more than just an episode in the history of the conquest of the Amazon. A few eloquent statistics: in the middle of the nineteenth century, the Indians represented a little less than 52 percent of the Amazonian population; today they make up only 3 or 4 percent. In the Putumayo valley, just a portion of J. C. Arana's "territory," the rubber frenzy cost the lives of more than forty thousand Indians. Occasionally, when the unpleasant news reached them, this troubled the consciences of a few Europeans: in 1910, the British government ordered its consul general in Rio de Janeiro to conduct an inquiry in the Putumayo; the shareholders of the Peruvian Amazon

Rubber Company wanted assurances that Arana had not committed the crimes attributed to him. Casement's report was damning, a long list of atrocities; James Bryce, British ambassador to the United States, commented upon this report: "It is no exaggeration to say that the methods employed in the collection of rubber are the most villainous seen in the civilized world in the last hundred years. The whip, fire, famine, all are constantly and deliberately employed, while rape and the worst brutality are inflicted on women and children in this cursed region, increasing, if that were possible, the horror of these scenes." This report, which was published at the end of 1913, was intended to put pressure on the Peruvian government. But has the situation of the few surviving Indians really been improved? It is probably more accurate to say that the collapse of the rubber market rid the Amazon of a good number of adventurers. The forest closed back on itself; it was returned to its original isolation, but without its original innocence.

PART TWO

Indians

PRIMITIVE
CONQUESTS

D O THEY POSSESS A
soul? Are they descended from Adam? The Indians still posed problems
even after they were proclaimed human. The question of their origin, a subject of speculation from the first, provoked a number of imaginative theories, inspiring many novels. But no Americanist could subscribe to these
fancies. The problem of the occupation and settlement of the New World
had to be worked out like a chess problem, with the Indians as pawns,
pushed into new territory....

PEOPLE FROM ASIA

It is generally agreed that man did not originate in America; rather, Asian
migrants moved there some twenty-five thousand years ago. This is the most
reasonable thesis and the only one—in a figure of speech dear to its defenders—that is able to satisfy the intelligent thinker. But while the shape and
placement of the two continents allow us to envisage such a simple solution,
one must still consider the scientific evidence. Georges Arnaud saw this as a
false problem raised by scholars. For him, all that was needed was intuition,
"simple perception." It is something everyone in the world has known for
ages; just look at an Indian, a live one or a photograph, and then at a Chi-
naman, any one, and then think five minutes about the face of the planet.

A family resemblance, no doubt about it. Add to that the Bering Strait,
providentially emerging at the end of the Ice Age to form a bridge between

the two continents, and the ethnolinguistic, ethnoprehistoric, ethnobiological, and, last, the ethnoethnological evidence. And the theory no longer seems fantastic....

We will not repeat all of the other theories, not the ones describing visits to the American continent by Phoenicians or Tartars or creatures from Atlantis, or the ones that make the Argentine pampa the cradle of the world's races. We will only mention a few theories whose authors have at least demonstrated a vivid imagination!

In 1571, the Spaniard Arius Montanus produced a scenario based on biblical texts: two distant descendants of Noah divided the New World; Ophis took Peru; Jobal, Brazil. A thesis that was taken up again by Bishop de Roo in 1900! In 1607, Gregorio García detailed the moral, intellectual, and linguistic affinities between the Jews and the Indians. For those writers who followed him, the Indians were the avatar of the ten tribes lost in 721 B.C. when the Assyrians conquered the kingdom of the Israelites. J.-C. Hervey of Saint-Denys focused his speculation on the Fu-sang, the area reached in 499 by the Chinese Buddhist priest Hui Cheng, before concluding that the tribes must be located across the Pacific on the west coast of South America. More recently, Louis Pauwels and Jacques Bergier advanced a theory that would have delighted Professor Challenger, the genius of the "Lost World": "We should not refuse to consider the possiblity of visitors from outer space, from atomic civilizations that disappeared without a trace, civilizations that had a level of skill and knowledge comparable to our own, the vestiges of science subsumed in the various forms we call occult theory."

People have a weakness for the bizarre and incredible. As rationalists (to some extent), let us, however, try to go back....

EIGHTEEN, TWENTY, OR TWENTY-FIVE THOUSAND YEARS

Traditional geology shows that the American continent was already in its present form at the time humanity first appeared on the earth; this means that population movements, if they were secondary, could only have been made along routes that are currently open: the string of Aleutian Islands and the Bering Strait. The ancestors of the American Indians followed that route fairly recently. The study of prehistoric geology leaves no doubt about that. Man passed that way no earlier than the end of the Pleistocene era. In 1932, a skeleton was unearthed from a fossil lake near Pelican Rapids, Minnesota; it was a complete skeleton of a primitive mongoloid type and was no more than twenty thousand years old. Additional evidence of man's presence in America—two types of weapons, Folsom and Sandia, found along with the remains of ancient bison—does not push this date back much farther. No more than the Sambaquis of Brazil. In these "garbage heaps of prehistory," mounds of shells and food scraps discovered along Brazil's coasts, José Emperaire and Annette Laming-Emperaire isolated two technically distinct layers representing two phases of population movement: in the oldest, only lithic tools, neither bone tools nor human skeletons, have been found; in the more recent layer, skeletons, tools made of chipped and polished rock, and whalebone sculptures. One layer dates from before, the other after, what is usually thought to be the optimum postglacial climatic period, about six thousand years before our time. Thus, the migrating hordes left signs of their passage along the entire length of their route, so that eventually we may find all the missing pieces of the American puzzle.

Ethnolinguistics, the study of human language and of exotic languages, provides a striking argument in favor of the Asiatic origin of the Indian; Edward Sapir was able to establish the relationship of languages in the Nadene group to those in the Sino-Tibetan, and Georges Dumézil, in a study comparing Turkish and Quechua, the Incan language, showed a similarity in the names of six of the prime numbers as well as in certain morphological and lexical elements. He concluded that, in all probability, Quechua and Turkish derive from a common parent stock, which became established in America eighteen to twenty-five thousand years ago and developed there.

That is well and good. But how can we explain the profound differences, cultural as well as physical, that separate the present-day inhabitants of the New World? How can we explain the coexistence of so many tribes speaking such distinct languages without introducing some vague idea of successive waves of immigration, without speculating on other factors, beyond the climate, that accentuated tribal differences still further? Paul Rivet was right in saying, "Between a Guarijo and a Botocudo, there are as many, or even more, differences in build, head shape, and facial features as there are between a Swede and an Italian, a man from Auvergne and one from England, so that one can no more speak of the unity of the American race than one can speak of the unity of the white race."

Rivet sees only one possible explanation for this mystery: interbreeding.

Without rejecting the theory of a basic Asiatic origin, he believes that new migrations took place in a more recent era; thus, Australians, Melanesians, Uralians—these last represented by the Eskimos—have contributed to the formation of the American population. A reasonable-sounding theory. Even though an exodus across the desolate landscape of the ice-free coasts of Antarctica gives us a sense of unreality and though the infinite expanse of the Pacific makes us lapse into a dream. (We do not consider the expeditions made by the *Kon Tiki,* the *Siete Hermanitas,* which was sailed by one man, and the *Tahiti-Nui II* to be sufficient proof. They are really no more than splendid athletic feats.)

THE ONLY REAL MEN

The men with slanty eyes moved into the farthest reaches of the Orinoco and the Amazon basin. "But this large isolated segment of humanity consisted of a multitude of societies, both large and small, that had very few contacts with each other," observed Lévi-Strauss, "and in addition to the differences caused by their separation, there are other equally important differences caused by their proximity: by the desire to distinguish themselves, to set themselves apart, to be themselves." Customs are born, sometimes out of internal necessity, sometimes by accident, but most often from a desire to be original and different. Significance ends at the boundary of the tribe or the linguistic group, and man recognizes as his equal only his brother and his own people. Even today, the tribes we call primitive give themselves names that mean "the only true men" or "the people," as opposed to "people." The Cashinahua Indians use *Huni-kui,* and the Guayaki, *Ache.* The names by which we designate them are usually no more than pejorative nicknames or the names of the places where they live, or perhaps just wordplay with no apparent meaning: the Inje-Inje Indians got their name from their neighbors, who claim that the Inje-Inje vocabulary consists of only these two sounds, with varying intonations and accompanying grimaces. The Indians known as Puinahua, "human waste," or those known as Chiriguano, "cold shits," would certainly choose a less disagreeable identity.

THE LARGE FAMILIES

It would be difficult to form a theory unifying these tribes into a harmonious whole, the Amerindian race or Atlantic subrace, or even one attempting to trace their tribulations through the skein of river systems, chains of lakes, and streams, without introducing an unacceptable potential for error. We would be approaching the darkest part of the ethnological night. But it is possible to track them mechanically: by ethnic groups, by languages and regions, by zones of influence, to attempt to chart the outlines, despite a bad map, a rigged compass, a broken sextant, of an imaginary country: the Amazonia of large tribal families.

The working hypothesis, then, is that the Amazonian enigma is contained in five family names: Arawak, Carib, Tupi-Guarani, Ge, and Pano.

At one time the Arawak must have been concentrated in the Andean piedmont. These peaceful farmers, who are also potters and weavers, were not able to resist the rise of the warlike Caribs, who took many of their women. Soon several groups of disheartened Arawaks fled to the north of Brazil; they dispersed along the Orinoco and the Rio Negro, some to the Antilles, others to the Chaco, where they were assimilated by the Tupi-Guarani. Today, they are on the way to disappearing, or descending into total *clochardization.** There are only a hundred or so tribes left, each with its own dialect. Some of these have been the objects of remarkable ethnographic works: the Mojo, studied by Alfred Métraux; the Paressi-Cabexi, by Lévi-Strauss; the Campas, by Stefano Varese; the Piro and the Culina. As for religion, the tribes of the Orinoco and the Rio Negro are characterized by the cult of sacred horns—enormous wind instruments played in the men's house—kept secret from the women; we have found these instruments among the Mojo in Bolivia. Most of the weaving of these tribes is done on vertical looms.

The Carib, whose name is the source of the word *cannibal,* are characterized by a taste for war and also for tobacco; they are known for their village festivals. In the Guyanas, where they have taken Arawak wives, observers were surprised to find a separation of linguistic function: Carib is the language of the men, Arawak, of the women and children. The men are hunters and fishermen, the women farmers who have domesticated numerous plants,

* Cultural disintegration, in which the Indians become *clochards,* bums and beggars (trans. note).

with agriculture being an exclusively female activity. Cannibalism is a religious practice. Add to that a passion for throwing lots, and the practice of couvade, and we have a portrait of the Carib customs.

Couvade, the mimicked pain of the father while his wife is giving birth, is also a custom among the Tupi-Guarani; but this childbirth drama is not unique to these ethnic groups, and the tradition of men struck down by labor pains has been found everywhere in the Amazon basin. It is necessary to look at other factors: does it have elements of messianic ritual?

Among the Tupi-Guarani, in fact, the shock of colonization favored the rebirth of ancient myths, and everything the tribes did seemed to be an attempt to arrest the growing social disorder by a return to indigenous values. The myths of the world-without-evil and the twins are the most common themes in this rather messianic movement, reflected in all of their oral literature. In short, because he knows that he is an Indian, the Tupi-Guarani has become an indigenist.

Between the sixteenth and the twentieth centuries, a tradition grew among the Tupi-Guarani of mystic activists, wearing priestly habits laced with crosses; they said that their mission was to lead the Indians to the world-without-evil, the place where true men would finally find redemption, virtue would be rewarded with happiness. In that land, man would never die. Why not fast to lighten their bodies, and dance, dance until the body lightened still further and became pure spirit? Why not follow the *pagés** to the heights or the ends of the earth so they might see with their own eyes the earth freely yielding up its bounty, the trees and fruits providing for man? Drawn forward by a waking dream, they continued their march as the days went by, one by one. Dazzled by visions, they were unaware of their misery. They truly were children of another century: oppressed by all the original sadness of South America, tormented by the idea of death, consumed by bitterness and utopian visions, they were the great romantics of the continent.

In eastern Brazil it was the Ge Indians who wandered the land. They had no weaving or pottery, no fermented drinks. Fishing for timbo fish, planting crops on burnt fields, creating and wearing labrets and beautiful feather arrangements, these are common to the majority of forest cultures; do all these Indians belong to some unknown family? The poverty of their material culture has made them marginal, but these raggedy paupers possess—a

* Indian name for sorcerer or shaman, a Siberian term.

fine compensation—a cultural system of beautiful complexity. The different groups (such as the Kayapo, the Xavantes, the Apinayé) do not observe the same rules, far from it; the only trait that unifies them—apart from language—is one also found in our culture: political clubs. These are groupings that go beyond the family and clan constellation, outside of all kinship ties; basically, the political clubs bring together individuals who share the same special interests, who are the same age or in the same situation. The marked opposition between married and unmarried men translates to a division into two "parties," a division that is somewhat illusory since it can be modified at any time, during the rainy season or in case of war, according to an arrangement in which style is redefined by deciding upon new rules. These decisions are made in the course of political assemblies in the *njobe*, the house of men and home of their culture. It is through the multiplicity of these interpenetrating structures, the complexity of their social life, that the Ge Indians respond to the contemptible fate of sleeping on the bare ground and living in hunger; they remind us of the true dimensions of the space of which they are still guardians: Amazonia, the world of will and reverie.

The Pano Indians, whose name recalls the Spanish mountain site of a heroic battle between Christians and Arabs, are scattered in the western part of the Amazon basin, where they have lived the life of hunters and semisedentary farmers since the earliest times. In fact, they often possess the charm of friendly peasants. Without flocks and plows. But peasants all the same.

(Honoré de Balzac, in *Le Cabinet des antiques,* noted this great similarity between men of the earth and men of the forest: "There is no one like the savage, the peasant or the provincial, to make a thorough examination of everything that concerns him; and when he moves from thought to deed, he displays much the same completeness." It is true of the Pano and other Indians. But seductive as it is, this "psychology" of savage thought seems too simple; a single mentality could not inspire two ways of life that are so distant in space and time. Peasants and savages are not rustic in the same way: the Indian lives off the earth, the peasant works it.

One common view is that the Indian is no more than a crude peasant, a blunderer, using primitive methods, and this inequality and artlessness link him to his tribe. The truth is just the opposite, it is the peasant who has sacrificed all richness to become an *unnatural* savage: he is productive, certainly, but the collective route to happiness is lost to him; his social life has no other meaning than work. And happiness? He no longer considers it within his province.)

Paradoxically, the reverse is true of life in Amazonia: unlike the French peasant, the Pano Indian does consider his own happiness. In fact, the Indians consider only happiness, regarding it directly and continuously.

Secluded and peaceful, they cultivate their gardens.... They have domesticated corn, groundnuts, bananas, sweet potatoes, sugar cane, pimento, dye plants ... and they know how to grow cotton, which the women spin and weave to make hammocks. Nature also works for them: the calabash plant gives them gourds and hollow bowls, the bees provide a natural sweetener, the bony tongue of the *pirarucu* fish becomes a manioc grater, and the jawbones of the piranha make an extremely sharp scissors....

It is true that not every need is as easily satisfied, and the Indians may not always be happy. But, living among them, we were surprised by the relation of these creatures and their world, their dreams, and their words; a subtle accord in which the soul is engaged in the moment. Theirs is not a perfect society, but it is harmonious and provides obvious pleasures. It seems satisfactory to us. Naturally, their problems, their difficulties, are enormous; they do not live as long as we do—their life expectancy is only about thirty-five years—and yet the life they lead within their small communities is so much more integrated than ours. Their existence provides a security, not a material but a psychic security, that is infinitely superior to anything we feel in our civilization. Alfred Métraux said of these primitives, "Man is infinitely less isolated than he is in the West." He added, "It pains me to realize that the last few civilizations that are still at this stage are rapidly disappearing. One of the greatest regrets of my life is that I have witnessed the death throes of so many of these small societies, *which we despise because when they are evaluated by the standards of our technology they seem despicable* [italics added], even though they actually possess a tremendous value and their disappearance will represent a profound loss."

But fortunately all is not lost. The Indians of the Pano family, for example, are still fine artists and honest craftsmen. And we must mention the beauty of Shipibo pottery, the richness and elegance of Marinahua weaving, the art of feather arrangement among the Cashinahua, the face painting of the Mastenahua, the originality of the flat hats and bark clothing of the Chacobo. But, above all, the consummate art is still that of the storyteller. The Indian legends, short fables, or novel-streams hold a captured beauty and poetry that their language supports wonderfully. Meteorological phenomena have an important place in these stories, because, we repeat, the

Indians are essentially farmers. Their words border on the parable. Listen to the very brief "story of the rain," in which the Cashinahua Indians let us catch a glimpse of the transparency of a world ordered by simple, everyday things: "Above us, in the sky, there is a lake with clear waters, a huge lake, and at the bottom there is a single hole where a bird nests. This bird sometimes leaves its home to go look for seeds and insects. When it is gone, the water runs out and waters the earth."

THE INDIAN ADVENTURE

We would be unwise to disdain savage thought, especially if in so doing, we invoke scientific thought, which does not itself disdain primitivism; we have witnessed an ethnologic panorama revealing the tremendous diversity of thought centered on the daily experience of nature, the careful reflection on man's fate in being born into a world that was not created for him. Primitive societies seem to meditate on their destiny, and their words and stories attempt to unite the spiritual and the physical, and to conciliate the forces of nature. And we have seen that each society has its own method, its own way of doing this....

But before it was home to a thousand and one cultures, Amazonia was a desert. A limbo of tree limbs. A distant planet, shimmering and rotting, where no man had ever set foot. Only a child could imagine it, because this forest reflected his mind, wild and melancholy. Truly, a supernature. It is unfortunate that the primitive hordes that came to the Amazon from the tundra and northern plains of Asia did not know how to write to provide a record of their conquest....

The Guayaki, like other Amazon Indians, have no memory of that period; but we believe that traces of it are contained in their story of the origin of humanity, the myth of *jamo pyve* (the first ancestors), as told by Léon Cadogan and Maxence de Colleville:

> The first men, they lived a long long time ago,
> Lived in the depths of the earth.
> They came out and went into the forest.
> They walked through the wild woods.
> All over the world, they came and they went.
> The first men had scratchy skin and stinky armpits.

With the advent of agriculture, weaving, and pottery, society takes a decisive step. From that point, men and women produce, they are *midwives* to nature. And even if primitive people were not destined to experience the great industrial convulsion, still it is no exaggeration to say that their discoveries loosed the bond of the imagination and freed progress.

What do we find on the margins of history? Only the Indian adventure. It provides us with tools. "The first men lived in the depths of the earth," say the Guayaki, perhaps suggesting that they came from "primordial darkness" to become the nomadic masters of the forest. The Bora Indians have a different idea of the first men; they tell us this: "Our ancestors were like the animals; they did not know how to do many things and they ate only what the earth gave them." In honor of the gift they receive from their god Betsé, the Cashibo Indians divide time into two periods: before and after Betsé taught them about agriculture.

It shows admirable courage for these cultures, which are always on the brink of disaster, to arm and defend themselves, plant and harvest, spin and weave, paint their bodies and chant poems.... In spite of death and danger, in spite of rampant poverty, they are touched by the glory of life; that is the Indian miracle.

It is a miracle too that these new Indians, armed only with sticks, almost without tools, were able to establish their families here, to find ways to survive in a forest where food is relatively scarce. Because, paradoxically, Amazonia is a land where man can go hungry. (Where is the super-Tahiti described by the amateurs of travel lore?)

The exuberance of nature is not a gauge of abundance and richness; just the opposite. The forest is restoring itself. It renews itself on a soil extremely poor in mineral salts, thanks to the furious activity of plants that sprout from dead leaves, trunks, as soon as they fall. Never-ending parasitism. Lowlands, floodplains, a world so poorly suited to the development of human life....

Above all, this environment raises the problem of stewardship. Among the Indians, the men hunt and fish, the women gather fruits, dig up roots, collect wild honey and larvae. But in the deepest part of the forest, the vegetation is so thick there are almost no insects, snakes, monkeys, and birds. A hunter can spend a day lying in wait for game and return to camp empty-handed or with no more than a partridge or a squirrel. The group cannot survive that way. A man can count on keeping himself alive by hunting; a society cannot. Most of the tribes very quickly established some sort of cooperative system guaranteeing that game would be shared; among the

Guayaki, for example, the hunter is not allowed to eat what he has killed; he must distribute it to his companions. Everyday etiquette, the gift from the hunt is the guarantee of equality among the members of the group and ensures the group's cohesion.

How did they move from the stick to the bow and arrow, from gathering fruit to agriculture, from hammered bark to weaving? By what route did they go from knotted palm fronds to basket making, and from baskets coated with wax to pottery? Here, imagination fails us. Lucky accidents, chance, cannot explain these finds; they require such complex operations, they must surely be the products of a determined quest; its progress may not have been scientific, but that is not to imply that it was blind. Agriculture, just like pottery and weaving, is the result of an incalculable number of trials, errors, and improvements.... If luck contributed to their development and if chance favored it, still, it seems to us that these "inventions" could not have been *completely* accidental (so we have preferred primitive "conquests" to primitive "discoveries"). About the cooking of food, Claude Lévi-Strauss wrote: "Some natural conflagration might perhaps have roasted or grilled food on occasion, but it is very hard to imagine how (except perhaps in the case of the eruption of a volcano, which occurs quite rarely) it could have boiled or steamed it. So, one would be wrong to exclude the inventive act, which was definitely required for these last methods, when attempting to explain the first."

Once chance and luck have been set aside, it is easier to see that the primitive Indians had a veritable "natural science." It is to them that Europe owes rubber, curare and cocaine, chocolate, potatoes, peppers, tomatoes, and bananas, among other things. Among the plants they developed are two that transformed the African economy: corn and groundnuts. Obviously, their contribution to the civilizations of the Old World has been considerable!

Little by little, the Indians were able to domesticate the forest.... They discovered the art of gardening, and this slowed their migration. In the clearings they cut in the forest, they grew the plants that they needed: manioc, in particular. This is why ethnographers have been able to describe the Indians as a *manioc civilization*....

Manioc cuttings are placed in the ground at the beginning of the rainy season, and with no more attention than regular weeding, the plants begin to produce tubers at eight months, continuing for a year and a half.

Despite the fact that manioc juice contains a deadly poison, hydrocyanic acid, Indians are able to make the bitter tuber edible. To do this, they remove the core from the thick roots, cut the roots into chunks, and soak them in water for several days to soften them. Then they crush them with a pestle. The resulting paste is placed in a rather unusual press: a long casing of plaited fibers, open at both ends, which the Tupi Indians call a *tipiti,* a grass snake. Two men stretch it, squeezing out all the poisonous juice. The residue, the cassava, is flattened to form little cakes and then grilled on a clay pan, to produce what might be called the bread of the tropics. There are variations on this process; for example, the Huitoto use a different type of tipiti: instead of being shaped like a muff, it is flat; the paste is carefully spread on it, and then it is closed up and twisted. The Ge use a different method to extract the poisonous juice: they grate the tubers, then place the pulp on a mat in the sun, where it is dried before it is baked. The Kubenkranken make their graters out of flat stones to which they attach fish teeth.

The number of different methods should not surprise us; each is a response to necessity—survival. It was a tough struggle; it still is. Nevertheless, manioc is not enough; it contains no vitamins or minerals; it is filling but not nourishing.

In spite of their bows, arrows, and blowpipes, their snares and traps, hunting does not produce enough food for the Amazon Indians. Fishing is more reliable: there are over two thousand varieties of fish in the Amazon, from piranha to pirarucu, and they can be as large as fifteen feet and weigh as much as four hundred and forty pounds; and there are also the crustaceans, the freshwater snails, and the turtles, whose meat is appreciated as much as their eggs. Generally, the Indians fish the same way they hunt: with bow and arrow. The tribes also fish collectively; the Motilones block a section of the river by building dams at either end, then they spear or club the fish trapped in the pool of stagnant water. Throughout the Amazon region, the Indians use *nivrée,* a method of poisoning the fish; they immerse pieces of poisonous vines, *timbo* or *barbasco,* in the river, and these release toxic substances that stun the fish, paralyzing them.

VARIATIONS ON FIRE

Hunting, shooting, and butchering game, these tasks always fall to the men; cooking is always the business of the women. Monkey and agouti roasts, stuffed fish, and braised bananas, grilled or boiled manioc, parrot giblets, well seasoned with red pepper, palm ashes sprinkled on as salt; occasionally, live ants or grilled grubs.... The Indian culinary art may make use of unfamiliar ingredients, but that does not mean it has no rules. It has a system of formal rules that ethnologists of the structuralist school have analyzed as they would a language. A grammar of "the raw and the cooked."

There is no society without cooking. Many Indian myths tell how the civilizing hero gave man the gift of cultivated plants and fire. Since it is not easy to start a fire, the Indians always keep some embers smoldering, always keep alive some hot coals. Without these, it is necessary to rub two sticks together; Helena Valero, a Brazilian woman who was captured by the Indians when she was eleven and spent twenty-two years living with Yanomami, tells how they make a fire: "They lay a flat piece of dry cacao wood on the ground, holding it between their feet; on top of this, they place a tiny stick of the same wood, which they twist very fast. After they rub it three times, the stick starts to smoke and a tiny ember starts to form in its pith; they drop this on a little chunk of *coupim* (termite nest) or on a few dry fibers. Then they blow, they blow and the fire takes hold." Among the Kayapo, a small piece of cotton, applied to the point where the two sticks rub together, becomes the kindling. Variations on fire.... The first men, with it, forgot their fear of shadows and wild animals. They burned so they could reap; they cooked their food. They dreamed.

The highest achievements of civilization were born from fire. Pottery emerges from it, fragile and beautiful. Like Indian society.

WAR, WOMEN, AND PEACE

IN TOUCH WITH THE UNIVERSE...

THERE IS ALWAYS A CERTAIN thrill at coming upon an Indian camp—the large collective houses of the Bari, covered with branches and palm fronds, or the Yanomami houses with thin mat roofs, joined in regular polygons.... There is a tremendous difference between these primitive hamlets and the cities where man imprisons himself in a confusion of neon and asphalt, concrete and stone. Indian huts, Indian villages keep a vital link with the universe; a hundred leagues away from our huge lifeless constructions are "the dwellings [of the Indians], which are large enough to be substantial despite their fragility, assembled as they are using materials and techniques that we belittle if we even know them; because these dwellings are not so much built as knotted, plaited, woven, refined and polished by their usage," wrote Claude Lévi-Strauss.

Along the trail of the nomadic or seminomadic life the Indians lead, the villages are only temporary stopping places. Subjected to slash-and-burn agriculture, the land that they clear is quickly depleted, remaining productive for only a few years; then they have to clear new fields and rebuild their camps near the new gardens.

With house and land passed from father to son, to the parish or a monument to the dead, it is material values that haunt the dreams of whites entrenched in their "little patriarchy." Real estate does not obscure the real Indian village, which is, more than anything, a cultural space, like a skeleton supporting a tradition and an ideal. Its form has a schematic function; the social and religious organization of the group is reflected there: the arrangement of the huts, the placement of the men's house, the location of the open space where feasts and ceremonies are held…. We will see how everyday activities are shaped by the design and at the same time the design is reshaped by memory. When the tribe moves, it is guided by a sure instinct and a sound practical science to reinvent itself without any change in the village layout, so that tradition is respected and good relations among tribe members are maintained.

LOVE AMONG THE INDIANS

The equilibrium of Indian society also depends on a complex system of family relations. Because the life of these "savages" is not as simple as we like to think. Judge from this: ethnologists have identified sixty kinship terms among the Bari, some of which express relationships as tortuous as "son of the brother of the wife of the brother of your spouse," "son of the brother of the wife of your son," and "wife of the brother of the husband of the sister of your spouse." … Some of these rules of Indian love appeal to reason: the laws of exogamy and the incest taboo, for example. Kinship restrictions have more influence on their lives than on ours. In choosing a wife, a man must take care not to violate any of the marriage rules. Generally speaking, a man must look for a future wife outside his clan or even outside his village. A wife can be procured from a neighboring group, with wives traded the way goods are exchanged. Sometimes it is just the opposite and the rules prohibit marrying outsiders; for this reason, Bororo groups have divided themselves into two "cartels," which give and take wives from each other. The arrangement of the village reflects this matrimonial organization, with each group living in a well-defined area. They do not have writing, but this method allows them to record the civil state….

The word *incest* among the Indians has a broader definition than it does under Western laws. Women are classified as marriageable or not according to a very strict system. A man cannot marry just anyone; even distant branches of the family tree may be forbidden, taboo. Some cousins are considered good marriage candidates, others are off-limits…. Each tribe has its own solution to the problem of marriage, intended to integrate all members into the tribal body and enable each to play a role. What is important is that each man have at least one wife.

The ideal of passionate love, which goes hand-in-hand with a certain possessive egotism ("The two of us, no one but the two of us," say the lovers) is not very strong among the Indians; the chivalric tradition has no equivalent in the tropics, and even in very Europeanized villages it is rare to encounter a couple who hold the faith à deux that inspires novelists to write romances. This is not to say that these people do not feel love. In fact, by a route other than free love or inflamed passion, their regulation of sexual need makes love a social activity. They try, for good reason, to eliminate passionate love, that is—here, we ask the reader to refer to psychoanalytic theory—they attempt to break with the cult of the mother. In this society, the role of the woman is diminished and the amorous quest is confined to its function: in most of these languages, the same word is used to denote eating and making love....

WOMEN DESCENDED FROM HEAVEN

This rigorous interpretation may perhaps exaggerate the subordinate role of women—they are exchanged, they are consumed—but it is true that in "the vaudeville of Indian love" wives play a very small part.... Most of the creation myths make this obvious: the women are useful, but secondary. Here is how the Toba of Chaco imagine a time before the advent of women, a time when men were not distinguished from beasts:

> At that time, there were no women; the men masturbated into calabashes. When the calabashes were full, babies came out.
>
> Every day the men went out hunting and left the meat from the day before on the roofs of their huts to dry. But while they were gone, the meat disappeared. They decided to leave a man behind to watch, but he fell asleep and did not see a thing. The next day it was the parrot's turn to keep watch. The men had not been gone very long before he saw women descend from the sky, by sliding down two long ropes, then seize the food and perch in a tree to enjoy their feast. Since their vulvas were studded with teeth, they fed above and below at the same time, ravenously.
>
> The parrot threw a piece of fruit at one of them, and the women

pelted him with all sorts of objects, injuring his tongue. When his companions returned to the village, he could not speak and could not make them understand what he had seen.

Then it was the sparrow hawk's turn to stand guard. He saw the women descend from the sky and throw themselves on the food. When they noticed him watching, they tried to kill him, flinging pieces of wood and hot coals at him. Then they started to climb back up into the sky.

But the sparrow hawk managed to cut one of the ropes. Several women fell from the sky, plunging into the earth. The sparrow hawk took two of them for himself and called his companions. The armadillo was trying to pull the women out of the ground by their hair to give one to each of the men.

The sparrow hawk warned them: "Watch out! Do not sleep with them, they will wound you with their vagina. Wait and I will make sure they cannot hurt you." But the fox did not want to wait: One bite and he was emasculated. Taking a stick of palo santo and two little round fruits, he made himself a new member. The next night he slept with a woman, who could not harm him.

In the morning, the sparrow hawk called up the wind from the south; it grew cold so they lit a fire. Shivering, the women crouched in front of it, their legs spread, to get warm. The sparrow hawk picked up a big stone and threw it at them to break their teeth; and from then on they were useful. To make sure they could do no damage, the armadillo penetrated them with his tail, which is encased in a shell. After that, they could all make love freely.

The first to impregnate his wife was the pigeon. But he was weak and his son soon died. And that is why the children of men often die when they are young....

If there is a strict law against marrying some women, there is no similar prohibition against marrying several. Only a dozen tribes practice monogamy, the Yagua among them. Everywhere else, a man can have as many wives as he can support; this means that a good hunter can have three or four wives. Most often, a man takes a second wife when the first gets old. The Shipibo and the Cashinahua customarily wed the sister of their first wife when they remarry. It is difficult for a Westerner to accept that this behavior, which inspires so many of our comedy routines, can be an accepted way of life among the Indians. For the Indian, polygamy has nothing of the savor of forbidden fruit; no lust underlies this multiplication of marriages. Having several wives is another way of adapting to environmental constraints: since they are responsible for gardening and gathering fruit, the wives add to the family's resources.

A marriage between one man and one or more women is not the only form of conjugal union. The Kaingang also celebrate collective marriages, which unite several individuals of both sexes into the same cell. Sometimes, as among the Guayaki, a woman can have several husbands. In short, any solution is good as long as it makes even a small improvement in the group's chance of survival, if no individual is injured by it.

Now that the population of these indigenous societies is declining, and the tribes are scattering and disintegrating, potential partners are becoming rare and polygamy is beginning to disappear. It is now the lot of only the most gifted hunters. Civilizing forces condemn the practice as immoral and would like to see it suppressed. Why? How can a Westerner, whose society produces adultery and prostitution, criticize the Indians' behavior?

Before an Indian man has the right to take a wife, he must prove certain things, especially that he is capable of taking care of a family. To do so, he moves into the home of his future father-in-law, and works with him hunting and farming. After this trial period, which can last a year or longer, his wife's family is able to judge his value and he has earned the dowry they will provide, having paid his parents-in-law in kind.

In most of these tribes, the young marrieds remain in the home of the woman's parents, at least until the birth of the first child. A Kaduveo boy leaves his family home when he is seven to go live in the men's house; at his marriage, he rejoins the opposite sex and goes to live with his mother-in-law. When a Kayapo man gets sick, he prefers to return to his mother's home so she can nurse him.... And what we have said about love is repeated here: the Indian spends his life extricating himself from the bonds that tie him to his origins. It also should be noted that Indians whose mothers have died are not so reluctant to adopt Western ways, which free the young couple from their guardians more quickly, allowing the husband to escape from the obligations his wife's family imposes on him.

COUVADE: A PSYCHODRAMA

In Indian camps one does not see the long strings of children that are the heartbreak of South American shantytowns. Indians have few resources; it would be impossible for them to take care of so many children. Everything, the nomadic life and the scarcity of food, calls for a restriction on births: In these nomadic and seminomadic tribes, Indian mothers bear only three or four children. Among the Nambikwara, the parents are not allowed to have sexual relations until the youngest child is weaned, that is, until the child is about three. Abortions are induced using medicinal plants and mechanical means. Infanticide is not unusual. A sickly or unfit child will not be allowed to live; they feel that he will not withstand the life awaiting him anyway. Twins too are sacrificed, because the Indians think they have evil origins and fear they are ill omens, portending some disaster....

Since the baby must be healthy to be allowed to live, the mother takes a thousand precautions while she is carrying it, trying to safeguard it from all sorts of malign influences. Even the father must take precautions so that he does not give the child the evil eye, causing bad fortune. They do not eat certain things: turtle, which would give the baby short twisted legs; howler monkeys, which would make it ugly and noisy; bananas, which would make its head soft.... The mother does not eat armadillo, because it carries its babies twelve months and she does not want to risk doing the same. The parents must respect these prohibitions and follow a strict diet until the child has "hardened," that is until it is one or two months old.

It is not unusual for the father to act the invalid when his wife begins labor, taking to his hammock and following a special diet. He is treated like a sick man. Sometimes he even behaves as if he is suffering labor pains. This practice, which is called the "couvade," is intended to distract the attention of evil spirits from the baby when it is first born and is most frail and weak, and therefore such a vulnerable target.

Even in those tribes that still exhibit elements of a matriarchal order—those where the child belongs to the clan of his mother, those where the young married couple takes up residence with the wife's group—the role of the head of the family falls to the father. Likewise, outside of the family group, power is never exercised by a woman. The tribal chiefs are chosen from among the most able of the community's men, often the most skillful hunters.

THE CHIEF IN PEACETIME

Montaigne asked one of the Tupi Indians brought to Rouen by a sailor what privileges were enjoyed by the Tupi chiefs: the right to lead the men into battle, was the reply. In fact, sixteenth-century travelers were astonished to discover that among the Tupinamba, there was ordinarily no single person who held power, that it was only when they went to war that authority was invested in a man whose skill and efficiency inspired confidence.

Even in our time, the Amerindian societies do not choose a chief, do not grant a man power to impose his will. Among the two hundred tribes of Indians scattered all over South America, there are barely a dozen—Arawak primarily—who have established a truly powerful chiefdom. In fact, the Jivaro vocabulary has never had a word that means chief. These scrupulously egalitarian societies are democratic in every sense, and the chief has only the power that the people concede him at any moment. Usually, the chiefdom is not a hereditary position; instead the chief is chosen by the influential members of his group and can keep his post only as long as he stays on their "good side."

More an arbiter than a judge, he is the moderating influence within the tribe, responsible for maintaining the group's equilibrium, which is always deeply threatened by any conflict that cannot find an outlet. It is even more important that he settle obvious quarrels than that he decide serious cases and complicated disputes. If the tribe is threatened by some external danger—war is a notable example—they need a stronger leader immediately. The chief often finds his power increased; occasionally, among the Cubeo and the tribes of the Orinoco, he cedes his position to a military chief, who returns it to him when the hostilities are over.

To be chief, a man must have one essential quality: generosity. Sharing is his most important duty. If an Indian chief were rich, it would lead to a loss of prestige, because he would be suspected of greed. He must be a good hunter and know animal tracks and where to find fruit and larvae, so that he can ensure the survival of the tribe in case of famine; when they are threatened by famine, the tribes of the Orinoco go so far as to take shelter under one roof. An Indian chief may well receive gifts, but he has no chance to hoard them; his tribesmen, the shameless beggars, press him to share his wealth; he would lose their favor if he refused.

The chief must make a speech periodically, in which certain topics recur, lofty themes of peace, honesty, and harmony. His talent as an orator allows him to function as the tribe's "peacemaker," encouraging his people to follow tradition and preserve their unity. Among the Nambikwara, the chief is called *ulikandé,* that is, "he who unites"; he represents the desire of the people to form a society.

Distinguished hunter and statesman, the chief usually has more wives than do other tribe members. Then, too, he needs the wives to help him meet the many obligations that come with his role. Nowadays, with the decline of the indigenous population, the chief is sometimes the only tribesman allowed to have several marriages. Still, it is hard to see this as a privilege or as a status symbol. As we have noted, his power is shaky: any slipup or setback would be held against him and he would soon find himself replaced by another leader. If a band of Nambikwara nomads feels that their chief is no longer any help to them, they will turn their backs on him and go join another Nambikwara group.

Never allowed to forget that he is accountable, the chief, in fact, obtains few advantages from holding this position, apart from the satisfaction of belonging to an elite (with the shaman and the elders). A chief cannot hold power by force, because his tribesmen keep a strict watch on his activities, and he must prove again and again, as much by his generosity as by his words, that he is not a threat to the equilibrium of the community; just the opposite, he is the tribe's guarantee of prosperity and security.

But since their contact with whites, this subtle notion of power based on mutual consent has begun to break down. The chief has become the intermediary between the civilized and the tribal worlds: he receives gifts from the whites, who treat him like some sort of Western despot. With the chiefs' cooperation, whites have been able to convince many tribes to emerge from their isolation and to live at the missions and white posts, and so take the first step toward giving up their traditional way of life.

WHEN WAR IS A RITUAL

Today's Indian chiefs have few occasions to demonstrate their valor and skill in battle; so few combatants are left that war parties are becoming increasingly rare.

The first travelers to the Amazon were struck by the ritual quality of Tupinamba military operations. "These barbarians do not wage war to conquer one another's lands and territories, because each side has more of both than they need; still less do the victors claim the spoils, enriching themselves with the arms and booty of the losers. They are not motivated by any other feeling—and this applies to both sides—than the desire to avenge their family and friends who were captured and eaten in the past," wrote Jean de Léry. The tribes maintain hostile relations with one another and every new incident calls for revenge.

Planned like any ceremony, like any feast, the battles, which occurred at regular intervals, fulfilled many functions in the life of the tribe. For young men, these battles provided an occasion to prove their courage, to show that they were truly men; for the chiefs, they were a way to gain prestige and power; and for the entire tribe, a way to gain wives, because the capture of women was often the motive for these excursions. Pierre Clastres observed that the Guayaki of Paraguay made almost the same preparations to meet a friendly tribe in a peaceful encounter where they would exchange wives as to launch a war party where they would capture them. "War is no more than a visit on an aggressive footing.... Peaceful visits are like a war that is prevented from starting. Hostile excursions and peaceful visits have the same objective: to obtain women." In the Tupi-Guarani language, the same word, *tovaja,* is used for father-in-law and enemy.

ANTHROPOPHAGY

Sixteenth-century French chroniclers left us detailed descriptions of the ritualized behavior that occurred during these explosions of violence. At the end of the battle, the prisoners were taken back to the victors' camp and their flesh was consumed ceremonially. Texts by Jean de Léry, André Thevet, Claude d'Abbeville, Yves d'Évreux, and Alfred Métraux provide lengthy analyses of ritual anthropophagy among the Tupinamba, who were the inspiration for the myth of the good Indian despite their cannibalism.

When they left for battle, the Tupinamba always carried ropes so they could bring their defeated enemies home alive. Capturing a prisoner was not an easy matter; it was a feat that made all the braves in the tribe proud. One man was seldom enough for it. But the captive became the property of the first man who touched him.

The victors returned to their village chanting and dancing; the prisoner, bound and tied, was mocked and abused. Enroute, his eyebrows and the front part of his skull were shaved, in the Tupinamba style. Then he was adorned with feathers and down, which were even stuck to his body, using honey or resin, and he was led to the grave of the man whose death was being avenged and whom he would replace in the community from that day on. In effect, he was no longer considered an enemy and became a "true man," the same title used for the other members of the tribe. Several days after his arrival in the village, he was given a wife, the widow of the man he replaced, or else a woman from her family.

The prisoner might be kept in captivity for a few days or several years. During that time, he lived just like the rest of the tribe, enjoying almost perfect freedom. Why, then, didn't he try to escape? "Heroes die in the enemy's camp," goes the saying. What greeting would his village give to a man cowardly enough to flee? If by chance he did escape, and then were captured, he would be killed and eaten at once, without any ceremony.

The prisoner might have been treated kindly, even pampered, but nothing could save him from the final sacrifice to which he was condemned. As for any children he might have had while in his adopted tribe, they would be considered enemies and sooner or later would suffer the same fate as their father.

When the tribal council, the *carbet,* selected the date for the ritual murder, the entire village would set about the preparations. They would braid the *mussurana,* the long cord used to bind the victim; fashion the club, the *ibirapema,* or *tacape,* with which to crack his skull; and prepare the fermented drinks that were indispensable at these celebrations. Some time before the chosen date, the prisoner was seized and shackled like an offender. "During this period," reports Claude d'Abbeville, "the dead man is avenged; everyone in the tribe is given free rein to hit and strike the prisoner, to pluck at his eyes and other parts, to visit upon him every conceivable form of injury."

Early on the morning of the sacrifice, the women prepared the condemned man. Washed, shaved, painted with genipa and urucu, he was smeared with honey and resin and decorated with feathers, down, and eggshells. Thus attired, he was led to the place where he would be executed. Around him were arranged all sorts of projectiles—fruit, stones, clay shards —which he would fling furiously at his enemies. In this agonistic ceremony, the victim was allowed his final symbolic revenge upon his executioners, in order to appease his spirit and guard against future reprisals.

Then the executioner would appear, painted with ashes and urucu, covered with feathers and jewels, bearing a red headband, the warrior costume. One of the tribe's braves would step forward and solemnly hand him the club he would use to beat the prisoner to death. The prisoner would attempt to avoid the club and even to seize it from him. When the victim finally collapsed, his body was carved up immediately and the pieces shared. The entrails, which were boiled, were reserved for the men, the women received only the broth. As for the rest of the flesh, it was dried and each member of the tribe received a portion, since the whole group had to participate in the agape.

Among the Tupinamba, cannibalism is a perfect form of vengeance. It is the strict application of the principle of reciprocity. When a man dies, it is the whole group that suffers, that is diminished. So the tribe must recapture the life force that has been lost. When one of their men dies, the Bororo, according to Lévi-Strauss, organize "a collective hunt ... a contest with nature that has a single object, killing a large game animal, preferably a jaguar, whose skin, teeth, and nails will constitute the *mori* (the price or fee) of the dead man." Anthropophagy is one of the ways in which indigenous societies attempt to compensate for their loss of integrity.

The act is religious, a sacrifice, to appease the soul of the deceased. Thus, it can be placed within the category of funeral rites. According to the sociologist Florestan Fernandos, the Indians believe that by eating the flesh of their prisoner, they acquire the energy of their deceased ancestor, for whom the victim is a symbolic substitute.

The ceremony completed, the executioner must perform certain expiatory rites and take several precautions to escape the spirit of his victim. The cleverest consists of changing his name, which allows him to elude his pursuer. After which, he has earned the title of *abaeté*, "true man," and can sit on the village council.

After the conquest, the Tupinamba were forced to abandon their warfare. Deprived of enemies and battles, they would go into abandoned cemeteries to dig up the dead; this way they could crack open the skulls, perform their rites, change their names, and become "men."

Ritual cannibalism was prevalent in the Amazon. During the sixteenth and seventeenth centuries, the Chiriguano Indians killed sixty thousand Chané in ritual executions. The Guarayu and the Huitoto were still cannibals at the beginning of this century. The Shipaia preserved the heads of their enemies in a hut, from the conviction that these trophies protected them from enemy attacks. The Parintintin devoured the eyes, tongue, and the leg and arm muscles of their enemies to keep them from seeing, speaking, walking, and shooting a bow and arrow.

In certain tribes, the funeral ceremonies honoring one of their own members include the ritual consumption of his remains. "When you die, no one will eat your ashes" is the worst curse that can be hurled at a Yanomami; among these Indians, the dead are burned in the village square and the ashes are, in fact, consumed by his family; if this is not done, the dead soul will be forced to wander endlessly, never finding repose. Raimondi reports that in Peru an old Mayoruna, converted to Christianity, was tormented by the fact that upon his death, he would be buried Christian style, feeding the crops instead of feeding his relatives. Some groups of Guayakis have also followed this practice of assimilating the remains of their dead relatives.

Under white administration, anthropophagy has pretty much disappeared, but the occasional occurrence gives rise to frightful stories about savage customs, which are used to justify vigilante raids.

There has been an effort to put an end to tribal wars, to "subdue" and "pacify" the Indians. But peace has not actually been established. Traditional enemies have just been replaced by a more cunning enemy: the white menace, with its naked lies and murders that are never avenged.

THE ROLE OF THE SHAMAN

Around 1920, the Mataco Indians were forced to give up their freedom: in response to continued attacks by Argentinian colonists who were trying to seize their territory, they placed themselves under the protection of the English missionaries who converted them to Protestantism. In exchange for a dull but secure life, they renounced shamanism, drinking, and war parties. Although the security they were offered was real enough, the Mataco could not adapt to their new life. They were "displaced persons." After a short time, there was a rash of suicide attempts, with the Indians trying to poison themselves with "sachasandia" fruit. It seems that the Indians were turning against themselves an aggression that they could no longer find a way to discharge in the puritanical and nonviolent society of the missions. Their behavior can also be seen as a symbolic protest.

In the Indian universe, where the sacred fuses with the profane in all things, the sorcerer is a person of considerable influence. For the pagé of the Tupi-Guarani tribes, the ethnologists generally substitute the Siberian term "shaman." Except among the Ge and the Guayaki, where no trace of it is found, shamanism occurs throughout the Amazon basin, but not in any very unusual form. The shaman's role is to communicate with spirits and, occasionally, with possessed beings; his art is performed in the service of the community in which he is the healer, the medicine man.

When a man is sick, if it is not an ordinary illness that some old woman can cure with infusions of herbs: the shaman is summoned to the bedside. The illness, in fact, could have been caused by an evil power that succeeded in putting the patient under a spell, which only the shaman can undo; or in capturing the victim's soul, which only the shaman can free.

Taking huge puffs on his pipe, the healer blows smoke on the patient in order to share a little of his own strength, at the same time that he vigorously massages the spots where small objects—thorns, darts, pebbles, or insects—are lodged. He claims these are the materialization of the source of evil. Gulping down a tobacco juice concoction, he starts to sing, to chant, and to shake his maracas to summon the protective spirits. Soon, the relatives of the sick person, who are outside the hut, hear noises, cries, and shouts: the spirits have come, the shaman is communicating with them. They denounce the enemy sorcerer, who is responsible for the illness, and so hasten the healing. Still singing and chanting, the shaman begins to extract the pathological objects, using suction. Some potion, some unguent—often one with real therapeutic value—and the treatment is done....

It takes talent to be a shaman, and a long apprenticeship. In some tribes— the Mataco, the Itonama, and the Mojo—women can be shamans, but their role seldom seems to go beyond that of bone setter or herbalist. In general, only men are privileged to be touched by a "revelation" that decides their career, either by chance, through a song or a vision, or by choice, after a period of fasting and ascetic practices. Except among the Munduruku, the role of shaman is seldom passed from father to son; in any case, the elect must complete his novitiate: he must spend a certain amount of time in semiseclusion, a period that may vary from a few weeks to a few years; during this time he will be subjected to a number of dietary restrictions as well as to both strict and partial fasts. He will be required to ingest bizarre beverages, hallucinogenic drugs, and brews of tobacco juice and bark that will make him vomit. All to make his soul light enough to join the spirits, and also to allow his body to be "visited" by them.

The shaman can heal a sick man, but he is also able to harm an enemy, making him sick, even killing him from a distance. His alliance with supernatural forces makes the shaman an object of fear (the jaguar circling the village may really be a spell caster preparing some disaster; in many Amazonian languages, the same word is used to denote jaguar and shaman).

His art makes him indispensable: he predicts the future, reads animal tracks; he is rainmaker, military adviser, grand master of magico-religious ceremonies. When the community is threatened, he is able to ward off the danger: during the smallpox epidemic that decimated the Pilaga Indians in 1932 and 1933, Alfred Métraux attended seances, exorcism rites performed by the shamans, who spent entire nights shaking maracas and reciting ritual chants intended to avert the plague.

The road to the world of the spirits passes through the state of ecstatic trance, and it is not surprising that mystics, the unstable, and even the simple-minded are predisposed to take it. But that does not mean that shamans are mentally ill, as is sometimes claimed. Nor should they be seem as frauds and fakers, as the missionaries would have us believe. Artifice and simulation are part of the scenario of healing ritual, of this ritual game whose power is no more doubted by the officiating priest than by his followers. Magic only works if one believes that it will.

Besides, when a shaman is sick, he calls his colleagues in for a consultation, proof that he believes in what he does. If he must know how to sing, and have a gift for imitations, for ventriloquism and prestidigitation, it is not so he can use these skills in the same way Molière's quacks use Latin. He uses his talents with all the seriousness that a good share of childishness inspires in him. He believes that his poetic and musical inspiration come to him from higher powers that have chosen him as their agent. As for the techniques that he uses in performance, the skills that he displays, he learned their ABCs in his childhood; while participating in the ceremonies that punctuate the life of the tribe, he automatically stored away much knowledge that was completed during his novitiate.

While they have traditionally been doctors, guides, and counselors, the shamans have seen these powers whittled away by the whites: Western medicines are promoted as more effective than exorcisms, and the Amazon's new diseases are not within the shaman's scope; the civilized world has made a fine game of exploiting these weaknesses to prove its own superiority. A shaman is not a shaman unless his community believes in him. But in rejecting him, the tribe loses a guide and a counselor; and at the same time they lose confidence in themselves and in their capacities for action and decision.

Once they have undermined the prestige of the shaman and have made their intermediary, the chief, indebted to them, the whites can boast of the clever way they have managed to pacify the tribes, who believe the whites' glowing promises and are ready to put themselves under the whites' tutelage, grasping at the illusion of an easier future. The whites tear down the village, change the environment, reform the structure of family alliances: opening so many breeches in a system that used to be coherent. It is hard to see what the West gains from this. It is easy to see that the Indians give up everything, getting nothing in exchange.

Even if he keeps his bow and arrows, his ornaments and body painting, the Indian smeared by Western propaganda becomes an exotic object, who can do no more than exhibit fragments of his folklore, flashy but worthless. Why should the whites exert so much effort for such a pathetic result? Is annihilation the real end of every colonization plan? The truth is that the humanistic zeal of the West has broken its word: it promised civilization and gave us the Third World.

CIVILIZATION OR CORRUPTION?

T IIE WHITE PRESENCE, artificially imposed on other cultures, creates a destructive and hostile climate. Wherever the white man settles, native society falls apart, dies out. This deadly pattern prevailed in the Amazon, and if it is hard to condemn the morality of the conquest—as a historical act it may have been inevitable and irreversible—we cannot be indifferent to its real cost. It would not matter if Philippe II had used the word *pacification* instead of the word *conquest,* it would not change the fact that what really occurred—and recurs in the case of the cultural and biological crime against contemporary Indians—was a rape. Cross-breeding, degradation, and genocide are the outcomes of this unfortunate contact.

THE CHILDREN OF COLUMBUS

The conquest was not a vast concerted movement; there was no colonial political structure governing it, at least in the early period. The conquest was composed of thousands of acts, and these were often separate acts. Motivated by a variety of ambitions, many of them conflicting: one man prayed for the natives, another preyed on them. It would be more accurate to speak of the different types of conquest, the territorial, the economic, the religious.... And the flower of Iberian virility, sexual conquest. With the inevitable effect, cross-breeding.

It goes without saying. The conquerors, after they had appropriated the land, could not coexist with the conquered population without exchanges between the communities. And, besides, the Portuguese sent unmarried men to America; they were not Puritans (like the English who came over on the *Mayflower*), and the Moorish occupation had acquainted them with the benefits of subject service. For them, love was color-blind: they cast their lot with the savage women.

Far from the city and its judges, the occupation troops had free rein to loot and pillage. The Indians were easy prey for the Spanish warriors, too. One custom spread from New Granada to Peru, the ordeal of the *capa plegada,* the rolled cape: Indian girls were wrapped in a cape and Spanish soldiers struck their "inferior contours"; if the girls collapsed, they were no longer young enough to be nubile; if they struggled, they were the right age to be delivered to the soldiery. These rapes produced the first generation of mestizos.

As the conquest went on, rape became less commonplace. The soldiers took concubines. For the Indian family, this meant an alliance with the conqueror, and for the children produced, an easier future. According to the Inca Garcilaso de la Vega, "When an Indian woman was about to give birth to the child of a Spaniard, her family gathered together to show their respect to the father, to pay homage to him as if he were an idol, in gratitude for his alliance with them."

On the Brazilian coast, a Luso-Tupi society was gradually established.

In 1510, Diego Alvares was shipwrecked off Bahia and rescued by the Tupinamba. The princess Paraguaçu was smitten with him; he married her and became the tribe's great white leader. When he returned to his native country, he took Paraguaçu, who had been christened Catherine in the meantime. They would enjoy a nice honeymoon in Europe—a plan still followed by Latin Americans—then return to Bahia to live.

Love and Mendel's law did the rest: the half-breed acquired the reputation of being the man in the middle. But because half-breeds were a new type, a new look, because there were not very many of them and they were unusual, the first half-breeds were arrogant and proud. Surely, being the child of a white represented an advance? Garcilaso de la Vega shows us the "privileged children" of Cuzco, proud of being twice lords of the land: their mothers were born to it, their fathers conquered it.

"The child of a Spaniard and an Indian woman is called a mestizo, to indicate that we mix the blood of two nations," proclaims Garcilaso. True, the mestizos enjoyed some privileges by virtue of the fact that they were not pure Indians; the sons of hidalgos, they felt they were hidalgos themselves (*hijo de algo,* that is, the son of somebody) and loftily refused to work.

But there was a hitch: since they were bastards, the Crown did not allow them to inherit from their fathers. They fell victims to laws of exclusion: denied property in the land that belonged to them as Indians, barred from access to the public employment owed to them as Spaniards; which led to resentment and occasionally to revolt. The mestizos, deprived of the privileges they felt were owed them, found that they were doubly outsiders, unable to share the life of the conquered people, and also unable to enjoy the life of the conquerors. Frustrated by their inability to achieve their white ideal, they attached themselves to opportunists and became their accomplices in the exploitation of the Indians. "The slayers of their mothers' race," say the first chroniclers.

Although they suffered different forms of abuse, the lot of the Andean mestizos was no better than that of the Amazonian caboclos: cast adrift, outside the culture, they left the countryside where they could no longer find a reason to live and took refuge in the suburbs of the cities, where this unsavory livelihood enabled them to remain idle. They were an object of concern among the Spanish authorities: they had grown so numerous that their status had to be defined; moreover, since they were outside the law, they did not pay tribute. According to Jorge Juan y Antonio Ulloa, "These countries have such abundant resources, and yet the mestizos do not do much—that is, they do nothing—none among them applies himself to work; instead, they lounge about, lazy and shiftless, cultivating nothing but vices; few of them ever marry and they lead a scandalous existence."

The Laws of the Indies represented a futile attempt to keep these "rough, immoral, thieving, gambling, vicious, faithless, lawless" creatures out of the Indian villages, to protect the Indians from the mestizos' actions, of course, but also to protect them from the mestizos' example.

POOR CREOLES

It was not only the Amazonian and Andean mestizos who inspired such uneasiness among the lawmakers; there were others "born in the colony," the Creoles, who gave the authorities just as much anxiety. In fact, the ties connecting the Creoles to the Old World quickly loosened. Not yet Brazilian, the Portuguese Creole was called a *mazombo*. The Spanish used the term *criollo*.

Born of European parents on the American continent, the Creole often went to Coimbra or to Salamanca to study, and once there he learned to his amazement that he no longer fit in the mother country. He did not even speak exactly the same language, and if he had the same religion and the same sense of family, there were enough subtle differences that he felt he was different. He had borrowed certain things from the native world: objects such as hammocks and the "grass snake" to prepare manioc; and words such as tomato, toucan, tapir, jerky; and fruits and vegetables, and plants such as tobacco, corn, potatoes; and other odds and ends of Indian culture, dispersed throughout South America, such as slash-and-burn agriculture.

The Creole dreams of Europe and scorns America. He flees the mestizos, chases the Indians, would like to tear the barbarians apart. Like his father. Let a play on words explain his misery: he is a postmature baby, a child born too late.

Ill at ease in Europe, he does not feel at home in America either. Like the mestizos, he is torn between two images, which gives him an excuse to conform to neither. Because he sees himself as different, he feels he is superior; he thinks he deserves certain privileges and wants nothing more than a golden sinecure. Failing which, he makes do with expedients, gambling and the lottery. Dissatisfied and dishonored, he is full of resentment.

"Mazombo, *adj.,* surly, dark, sad," say the dictionaries. Imprisoned in his resentment, incapable of finding a role fit for him, how can he not feel gloomy and unpleasant? In Peru, the criollo is the braggart, the man with big ideas, who runs away when he is called upon to act. As for *criollismo,* it includes every kind of irresponsibility. The interminable lines at the bus depot? "That is our criollismo." The labyrinth of bureaucracy? The chaos of local government? Criollismo strikes again. Excused with an indulgent smile, as if dismissing a collegiate prank. It is true; he is an overgrown adolescent; mazombo or criollo, he is the person who believes more in chance than in progress, who never makes the tiniest decision, who holds no ideals and so is motivated only by self-interest and the desire for glory, which must also provide some immediate benefit. Uncomfortable in his native land, he behaves like the demanding guest who lingers on refusing to leave, often putting on a show for the gringo, whom he envies but does not like.

The whites—although they represented the ideal of the creoles and the mestizos—did not make a very strong showing in Amazonia. For years, they did no more than pass through the jungle; it did not tempt them enough to inflame an ambition to stay there. In 1857, a German group came to Peru, settling in the Ucayali region, to build a colony modeled on the lands of Posuso. The area was said to be fertile. Thirty years later, Colonel Pedro Portillo was touring the province and came upon their village. He was horror-stricken: starving, sickly, in rags, the colonists were mired in a life of penances, rosaries, and litanies, victims of a crazed fanaticism. The group had been practical and efficient when they arrived; the climate and the isolation had driven them mad. Another example: at the end of the Civil War in the United States, some Southerners sought refuge in Brazil. One of their groups had gone to settle on the right bank of the Tapajos River, in Santarem. In 1940, a journalist searched for them and could find no traces. They had disappeared, except for two survivors, who looked just like the caboclos with whom they shared their life, following an ancient rhythm and smoking the same pipe. There, too, the West had rotted away.

During the Nuremberg Congress in 1936, the Third Reich made plans to obtain a monopoly on South American petroleum and to send the Fifth Column to launch an assault on the jungle. The project was called off, but imagine what might have happened to the impeccably disciplined Nazis if they had gone to the Amazon. Would Amazonia have destroyed them like all the others?

When whites leave the cities, with their familiar rhythms and perspectives, they tend to lose their traditional ways of life and and eventually adopt native customs. The establishment of a strongly centralized government during the colonial period should have prevented the spread of this degeneration; at least, that was the theory. However, in the mixed villages, ordinary whites, artisans and peddlars, and ignorant preachers ended up resembling the mestizos for whom they were the models (the Indians had already placed themselves at a distance). Thus, a mixed society was formed; fairly homogeneous, it was a rough draft for today's South American middle class. "We are not Europeans, we are not Indians," wrote Simón Bolívar, "we are midway between the natives and the Spanish." It may have been a new society, but it was still a daughter of Europe, which had established its social, political, and religious structure. And what place did the Indian have in such a society? Wasn't American man just a new form of Western despot?

INDIANS NO LONGER INDIANS

In their encounter with civilized man, the Indians lost too much and gained too little. They became dissatisfied with themselves and their culture, and let themselves be overwhelmed by modernity. Passively. In Brazil, Portuguese colonization produced two types of communities: the original Brazil, a traditional region including Amazonia and the inland area; and modern Brazil, on the Atlantic coast, a Westernized region that has long had a mixed population of blacks and mestizos. So that within itself Brazil contains master and slave, the colonizer and the population he oppresses. In Brazil, but also in Bolivia, Peru, and Colombia, the Amazonian hinterland is exploited like a colony. Disoriented, the Indians let themselves be seduced by the glitter of coastal civilization, completely unaware of their segregation in the heart of the land. They abandon their traditions to become strangers to themselves, to become victims of alcoholism and epidemics, of prostitution and charity. They are society's rejects. Today, the countries involved are asking themselves, a little too late, if they have not fallen victim to a cheap trick: don't they need these "de-Indianized Indians"?

The destruction of the Indians of the Amazon basin is like university reform: it has been talked about ever since Montaigne. Let us establish one fact: there has been no meaningful change. Researchers have raised a number of questions and have described a useful concept, that of acculturation. The word is not very pretty, any more than the process it describes: Composed of *ac* (toward) and *culture,* the term acculturation refers to a change, a transfer; it is the adaptation of a population to a culture that is new to them.

The Amazonian tribes knew nothing of the West but violence and religion; the first contacts, which were friendly, even enthusiastic, were spoiled by the intolerance of the agents of civilization toward these people who were not "men of reason" (meaning "Christians"). In the name of reason, the indigenous peoples were displaced, by force if necessary. Death or cultural suicide, that was the choice they were offered.

This did not disturb the white peace of mind. Humanism is smugly self-righteous, affirming its own values and rejecting all others as entirely outside the realm of reason. And, to quote Pierre Clastres,"It is in light of this twin aspect of the West, its full image, that one must view its relation to primitive cultures: the actual violence of which they are victims is not separate from humanism, it is just the visible sign of reason carried to its farthest extreme; and under its mask, this twin aspect defines our culture. It is as if our culture can only organize itself against what it has named the unreasonable."

On the edges of reason, like children on the borders of a free adult society, the madman and the savage share the same exile. Enigma or obstacle to our understanding of man, they are equally dangerous, creatures to be excluded or destroyed.

Feeling this odd kinship, Antonin Artaud made a trip to the land of the Tarahumara, but the West distorted his attitude and his responses to it: "They live in defiance of the world, they do not speak of progress, no doubt because they have despaired of achieving it." His error was in seeing the Indian as no more than an aspect of man, man as damned creature. In fact, the Indian has his own way of being human. A human being!

To the areas where its empire was not yet established, the West sent increasing numbers of emissaries, soldiers and missionaries; the generous impulse to impose its cultural models. The Indians lost their high spirits and their health, but isn't the happiness of others worth a little sacrifice? Happiness? Well ... the conqueror's hope of acquiring it someday...

And the Catholic and Protestant missionaries laid siege to Amazonia. Zealous proselytizers, they spared neither money nor energy to preach their biblical message. The Indian religions are "open" (syncretic, as the ethnologists say) and the Indians are often willing to welcome unknown gods, but the Christian god is a jealous god, an exclusive god. Letting him into the heart of the coherent universe of indigenous societies often results in the destruction of their harmony. So that converting the Indians begins a slow death.

Not long ago, the Indian scorned competition, profit, advancement ... because he was not individualistic. He was skilled at living communally, following the rhythms of nature. But the new order forced changes, upsetting man's relationship with nature, but especially man's relationship with his fellow man. Today, if there is any solution, it cannot be an individual one. The native Americans have been caught in our trap: the Indian can never fill the gap between his production and his needs. We will not dwell on how the actions of church and state throughout the history of the white invasion of America combined to destroy the indigenous world. Displaced, dispersed, indoctrinated, the Indians had new religious, social, and political structures imposed upon them, a new system of values. In Brazil, the vernacular languages were replaced, either by lingua geral, or by a pidgin Brazilian or Spanish. The Indians preserved their traditions in scraps of their material life, of their folklore. What does this pitiful remnant mean compared to what was lost?

Curiously, the colonial society only acted as a barrier to the Indians' access to the better world that it pretended to open to them. As a result of segregation and discrimination, the Indians were gradually overwhelmed by feelings of impotence and inferiority, which seemed to prove that the white man was right, he was stronger. Demoralized, they became resigned to this aspect of their fate and became the beasts of burden needed by the colonists. Many of us would say that none of this has changed in our era. Whether through brutality or stupidity, the Indian is always sacrificed.

For the missionary, the Indian is a pagan who must be converted, that is all that matters. So the missionaries pursue their work of evangelization indiscriminately, in contempt of the indigenous cultures that they demolish bit by bit. (It is not a question of whether the teachings of the Church are good or bad, but whether they are beneficial to the Amazon.) It must be granted that the missionaries occasionally come to the aid of their flock, preaching against the abominations of adventurers and exploiters; just like the earlier missionaries, Bartolomé de Las Casas and the Jesuits of the conquest period, these priests and pastors never stop repeating that the threatened populations have a right to life. Why do they do it? By distorting their passions, their habits, their beliefs, they are no doubt trying to create the illusion that the Indians are Brazilians (or Colombians or Peruvians...). But the Indians have no notion of the Western worlds, so there is no way they can enter it and find happiness, and they are soon on their way to ruin. Is this the true spirit of the sacred texts? Is this the meaning of the message that they teach? The members of the New Tribes Missions or of the Linguistic Institute of Verano show admirable determination in their travel throughout Amazonia. Their goal? To learn the indigenous languages so they can translate the Bible and rewrite the ancient words. Valuable work for ethnologists and linguists, but it announces the end of still more human groups. The advance-guard missionaries often entrap the Indians, and yet the ministers of the cult are certainly acting in good faith: the Indians come to them seeking refuge from adventurers, or looking for food or medical care. It is then that the big farmers or the rubber companies take advantage of their naïveté to recruit their labor.

In Peru, near Iquitos, the Canadian missions have established their general headquarters: church, hospital, schools, both primary and technical, a radio station. The children who attend the schools in the mission are boarders. What future do the missionaries hold out to these children, who are no longer taught how to live according to local wisdom? A miserable life in some shantytown or on a hacienda in some hovel crammed with peons?

POISONED GIFTS

The Indian problem requires kindness and courage, but especially knowledge. Bertrand Russell emphasized this challenge to virtue: "In the Middle Ages, when plague appeared in the land, pious men counseled the population to gather in the churches and pray for its disappearance; this resulted in the disease spreading with an extraordinary rapidity among the supplicants thus assembled. This is an example of love without knowledge." The last war provides an example of knowledge without love. In both cases, the effect was death on a grand scale. However much goodwill, however many good intentions inspired their creation, the many agencies dedicated to upholding Indian and tribal rights have nevertheless contributed to their decline. Poorly conceived charity has ruined the Indian.

The first blunder: germs have killed more native Americans than guns. Gilberto Freyre has very aptly called this "Western syphilization." The Amerindians, just like the Trobrianders or the Maori, are vulnerable to even the mildest diseases; there is no point in attempting to list the shocking ravages caused by the outbreaks of measles, smallpox, and influenza. However long we went on, we could provide only a partial list. We will just cite the case of the Bari Indians: during the four-year period between 1963 and 1967, ethnologist Robert Jaulin estimated that nearly 50 percent of the tribe was destroyed by disease. (From the standpoint of culture and linguistic diversity, it is as if half the French had disappeared one day....)

Westerners have often brought Indians the gift of domestic animals, usually chickens and dogs. As a token of friendship these are useless and can even be dangerous, since these animals carry germs and create filth in the Indian camps.

As for the clothes in which our modesty wishes to cloak them, what could be more ridiculous? In the forest, what could be more cumbersome and unnecessary? Bad even when they are not fatal, as they were in Tierra del Fuego, where the hunter-fishermen wore only animal skins over their nakedness and withstood the frosts of winter fairly well. After clothing was distributed to them, they were decimated by pneumonia, which they contracted while shivering in their waterlogged shirts. Clothes make no sense in the tropics either. "It has frequently been noted," said Étienne Dennery (speaking about Asia), "that when people who are used to working seminaked begin wearing clothes regularly, they are more susceptible to hunger and disease." The weakening that results—a sodium chloride deficiency caused by perspiration—is the prelude to a deadly disease: tuberculosis. Moreover, the Indians have other equally effective ways to protect themselves from insects and exposure to the sun. Painting their bodies with urucu and genipa is certainly a better response than ours to the need for elegance and protection from the elements. Even the smallest gift can have grave consequences for the life of the group. Beads, scraps of fabric, cooking pans, and manufactured goods in general signal the gradual loss of their own crafts. Eventually, their renunciation. Why spin, if one can obtain a canvas bag and some cheap fabrics? Why knead and shape clay, if tin containers work just as well? This is unfortunate for collectors of folk art, of course, but it also has a more serious consequence: it decreases the Indians' pride and independence and increases their needs so that they soon fall victim to the jungle traders.

It is generous to distribute foodstuffs to the Indians, but consider the consequences, which may well be bad in the long run: having received rice or corn, the Indians may neglect to plant their crops; then the next year, they will suffer from famine or at least food shortages.

Nothing can be introduced to the tribe that does not somehow affect the structure of their traditional needs and activities. A comb will be exchanged for a comb. Go no further. Never forget: for the Indians, exoticism is a fatal disorder.

HALF-LIGHT AND PSEUDO-SILENCE

When indigenous peoples are driven by disease or persecution to take refuge with the whites—missionaries or sympathizers—they usually find themselves lodged in unhealthy settlements; in the mission of Upper Catatumbo, Father García Herreras attempted to house all the Bari Indians from the Colombo-Venezuelan border in barracks made of corrugated tin.... That is to say—rather than provide a decent home or even help them to build their own homes—we sought to put them in a setting as different as it could possibly be from their traditional home. It is no figment of the traveler's imagination; primitives do organize their domestic space in certain

ways: whether it is in a circular village with the men's house as pivot
(Bororo), in a collective dwelling (Bari), or in a camp that reflects the sexual
division of daily activities (common among nomads like the Guayaki).

Claude Lévi-Strauss wrote, "The circular arrangement of huts around the
men's house is so important to the social life and activity of the group that
the Salesian missionaries in the region of Rio das Gracas quickly learned
that the surest way to convert the Bororos is to make them abandon their
village for one where the houses are laid out in parallel lines. Disoriented
without their village compass, deprived of the village plan that reinforced
their knowledge, the indigenous peoples quickly lose their sense of tradition, as if their social and religious systems were too complicated to survive
without the schema manifested in the layout of their village."

The Bari Indian house, as described by Robert Jaulin, shows the same
regard for order and function. Sixteen to fifty feet high, thirty-three to one
hundred and thirty feet long, twenty to sixty feet wide; these dimensions
vary according to the number of people it will house. It takes about a fort-
night, or sometimes as much as a month, to construct this work of art, with
the entire tribe participating. In its center, a very large space is reserved for
the kitchen, set off by a woven partition with openings to provide access.
Around this nave is an aisle like an ambulatory, a passage hung with hammocks, with each family occupying a particular section. In the kitchen there
are stone hearths, usually eight of them, and meat-smokers, and woodpiles;
this is the center of communal life. The entire house is bathed in shadow,
which keeps the mosquitoes away and makes it a wonderful refuge in the
heat of the day; those who have work to do—women who want to weave—
go to sit against the outside wall where light filters through the weave of the
basketwork panels. (The Bari house reminds us of all houses. A house for
dreaming and sleeping, for eating, for making love.... A house that civilization's game would like to replace: with cinema, hotel, restaurant....)

The Bari house feels like a special place: there is the odor of cedar, the
heaviness of the air, the half-light, and pseudo-silence.... It breathes with its
own rhythm. What will become of the group, far from their home? Without
mentioning the discomfort of the too-hot barracks, where the light is too
crude, where the cement floor is too hard, because the women—for example—cannot plant their looms in it to weave.... The Bari Indians provide a
simple image of happiness, warm and welcoming: something to eat and *their*
house around them. To deprive them of these two things would be to kill
them.

GOVERNMENT AND THE INDIAN

It started with their reception by a few whites who were not "deterred by generosity." In 1955, bad weather damaged the palm trees of "Serra dos Dourados": driven by hunger, the Xeta Indians left the forest for the first time and went begging for food from the owners of the "Fazenda Santa Rosa." The manager, Antonio Lustoza de Freitas, received them with so much courtesy and consideration that they did not hesitate to apply to the Service for Protection of Indians (SPI) What happened? In 1963, the ethnographer Loureiro Fernandes declared the group extinct.

What becomes of the tribes that come under the protection of the Indian protection agency? The "pacified" Parintintin are no more than poor caboclos, dressed in tatters, reduced to begging. The "pacified" Kaingang languish on a reservation in the state of São Paulo where the Indians condemned by common law are kept penned up by the Brazilians. The "pacified" Maka from the Paraguayan Chaco now live in the zoological park in Asunción, where they "play the Indian" for spare change. Is this the price the Indian must pay to become a member of the national community?

The Mexican experience gives us grounds for pessimism: "The Indian is Mexican," writes Alfonso Caso, the director of the Instituto Nacional Indigenista de Mexico, "because he pays taxes on his sales when he travels to market towns to sell his products or to buy the goods he does not produce himself; he is Mexican when he signs up to work on the coffee or banana plantations, where he receives an advance on his salary in the form of a large dose of alcohol, which stupefies or sickens him; he is Mexican when he falls into the hands of the municipal police who throw him into jail to make sure he pays his fine and, since he cannot, force him to sweep the village streets the next morning; he is still Mexican when he pays taxes indirectly every time he purchases the goods the shopkeepers of his village sell him at inflated prices. But when his community is struck by an epidemic of typhus or smallpox, he has no doctor or Mexican medicine to cure him; cultivating his patch of land or his mountains, he gets no help, neither aid from Mexican technicians nor credit from Mexican banks; as for teaching his children, there are no Mexican schools for them; finally, if he wants to leave his isolated community, cut off from any communication with the rest of the country, he will find no Mexican road passing through his village."

Indian tribes do not live by the same rhythm that we do; as soon as we force them to obey our sense of time, we have established a relationship of dominator to dominated. They are thrown off balance immediately. With their rhythm denied, the songs that sustain them forgotten, they can no longer align themselves around specific values. Some of them want to adapt to the new rhythm—those of São Paulo or of other cities where night no longer follows day—but soon they suffer the reversals forced on them by a radically different system, an economy that is never satisfied, and they renounce the illusion of power and come to their senses: too late! Nostalgia for the old ways is a reaction to *Indianness* lost. For them, the circle of the large family of man is a vicious one....

When the governments of Latin American countries are powerless outside the capital and the largest cities, as is usually the case, the only authority is the "local dictator." So the Indians become the favorite targets of opportunists—with all their abuses. Most notable among their exploiters are the petty traders who extort animal skins, forest products, and "folk" objects from the Indians in exchange for cheap merchandise, fabric, the basic "consumer goods" of the national market. Gradually strangled by this trade economy, the tribes grow poor and finally disappear. Societies without writing, without machines, are also—and this is not only a consequence but a fundamental principle—societies where man does not exploit man; they are thus powerless against mercantile colonization.

Sometimes groups of Indians become the prize of a tourist company: then all they have to do is put on a show and throw together some "folk" souvenirs. On the island of Bananal, an air-conditioned hotel is being built for the tourists who want to visit the Karaja Indians. The clay figurines the Karaja traditionally made are very popular with the tourists and so the Indians have stepped up production; now they turn out more statues, but they are less beautiful and lack religious value....

The Shipibo of Ucayali, who supply the shops in Pucallpa, no longer make bows of *chonta*: why should they? It is so much easier to work in soft wood. As for their technique, it has become hasty and crude. Their ceramics used to be the most beautiful in the Amazon basin, but now they have none of their old workmanship and the decoration is uninspired....

Their corruption seems to be the result of an illusion: the Indians are trying to live in two keys, ancient and modern. At the same time. But the Indians appreciate only the simplest traits in our culture, the ones that are —unfortunately—the weakest. They add these traits to their own culture without integrating, interpreting, or changing them. In this way, they create hybrid societies that are unlivable. Their passive resistance is not enough to sustain them, and they gradually lose even a sense of the injustice that is crushing them.

The Indian is defined by membership in a community that is held together by language, traditions, beliefs, and obligations. In this reduced space, the community displays all the characteristics of a society and it expresses all the social and cultural forms of man. Nothing is given within this community, everything is constructed: if one detail of the system is altered the entire system collapses.

Cultures that are integral wholes, fragile cultures: any adulteration ruins them. People tell us that we cannot seriously wish to protect these cultures, because—sooner or later—they will be threatened and they will succumb, swept away by the monstrous tide of the West.

"Be realistic!" say the experts on Third World affairs. We are being realistic: once these Indians are lost, how can they be replaced? And so, the words of the technocrats need to be expanded and clarified: our meeting with the Indians, have we set it up because we want the laggards to get in step with us? And is it a meeting or a trap?

GENOCIDE IN AMAZONIA

W H Y A R E' T H E majority of Westerners unmoved by the death of the Indians? Is it that, as children and adults, we have dreamed of them too often? So that now their death—in like manner—seems unreal to us. An imaginary life, imaginary death ...

Two press clippings, sixty years apart, should give us a taste of reality:

JORNAL DO
COMERCIO DE MANAOS
Saturday, 14 September 1907

ATROCITIES IN COLUMBIA
Indians—men, women, and children—are being tortured in the centers of rubber production.

LE MONDE
6–7 July 1969

BOGOTA, 5 JULY 1969 (A.F.P.)
Quoting a statement by Mgr. Geraldo Valencia, Archbishop of Buenaventura, the Colombian newspaper *La Republica* revealed Thursday that seventy-five Indians were sold by rubber dealers along the Colombia-Brazil border for the sum of 140,000 F.

Unlike the problems of starvation in Africa, upheaval in Eastern Europe, conflict in the Middle East, discrimination against blacks, or even the slaughter of baby seals, the genocide occurring in the Amazon does not attract much public outcry. The death of the Indians does not disturb Europeans since the superpowers are not involved and the UN has not stepped in ... The events in Amazonia seem to be no more than the operation of the law of the jungle. And then, compared to what happened in Vietnam, the massacre of a few primitives scattered throughout South America hardly seems to have more than sentimental importance.... In fact, an entire segment of humanity is moving toward destruction, and the international audience—which calls for justice in many less urgent cases—is watching as unconcernedly as if it were an ordinary event.

The left-wing press is silent. For a simple and disturbing reason: what is happening in Amazonia does not fit into their standard dialectic. Who are the imperialists and the anti-imperialists in this affair? The right-wing press speaks of the slaughter cautiously; is it in favor of the genocide?

Both of them balk at scientific articles. As if anthropologists wanted to stop the course of history! For journalists, the massacre of Indians is just "an old chestnut," to use their own slang, that is, a subject that can be written up year after year when there is nothing very sensational in the news and the newsmakers have to dig up ancient topics to keep the interest of their readers; and so, genocide inspires no more than the same sort of tired platitudes written about car accidents, cancer, the pill, and LSD.

RUBBER KILLS

The truth is that the Amazonia of the oppressed has never had an audience. After an article appeared in the Manaos newspaper in 1907, it took seven years for the closure of the Peruvian Amazonian Rubber Company, the company responsible for the rubber zone in question; it took seven years for public opinion to admit the truth of the accusation, to shake the disbelief that is the guarantee of a clean conscience; the society rests on the most wretched system of exploitation of the indigenous peoples, which leads quite logically to the extermination of the Indians in the Putumayo valley.

The disparity between the opposing forces makes the idea of genocide seem absurd: what connection can there possibly be between Julio Arana, the distinguished businessman who speaks English like an Oxford graduate, and the Huitoto Indians he is murdering? Doesn't this lord of the rubber industry have a little savage boy—a Huitoto, in fact—living with him in his London mansion and doesn't he even plan to send him to a university? If a few criminal acts are perpetrated from time to time, they must be the work of abusive foremen, without the knowledge of the company's owner. An argument that calms the London shareholders and removes any taint from the profits they stow in their safety-deposit boxes.

In fact, Indians in exploitable areas were enlisted by company recruiters: seduced by splendid promises or chased down and captured by force, they are mustered in rubber company headquarters, well-defended fortresses at the confluence of two rivers. Then they have little hope; they are condemned to produce more and more rubber and to die from hunger and abuse. The power of their master is symbolized by the "mark of Arana": when they do not produce enough rubber, the Indians are flogged with heavy whips, big around as a thumb and made of tanned tapir skin, and this flogging leaves them with hideous scars, the mark of Arana. At the garrison at El Encanto, the Huitoto are forced to work sixteen hours a day; their entire salary is a single meal, a bowl of manioc gruel and a can of sardines split four ways. In the forest, they tear up plants, leaves and branches, in an effort to appease their hunger. Forced to travel several miles carrying balls of rubber that can weigh more than ninety pounds, they stumble along under the watchful eyes of overseers who bully and harass any stragglers. All around this station Hardenburg saw prostrate Indians in agonies of pain and fever; they are left to rot on the ground without so much as a glance; one guard commented that some days "the stench was so bad it ruined his appetite."

To head these stations, the company hired hardened criminals, men who have proved their brutality. The employees who are hired, whites and mestizos, take one of two positions on the "cleanup" teams: either rounding up Indians in the forest or hunting down and punishing runaways. Escaped workers receive the same treatment as runaway slaves. At the garrison of Ultimo Retiro, Daniel Collantes, who refused to obey orders, was thrown into prison and sentenced to receive one hundred lashes, from which it took him seven months to recover. The company hired Indians from Barbados to handle police and guard duty; they fulfilled their duty as mercenaries under threat of execution.

As for all the young Indians of the valley, they were trained to denounce and to kill their elders.... This general complicity was a guarantee of the obedience and silence of all, ensuring the company's impunity.

The law of the jungle was to carry sadism to ever greater extremes. "These are not men, they are animals," their masters said of the Indians. One day the manager at the garrison in Abisinia ordered all the young children to be gathered together and beaten and then cut and thrown to the guard dogs, which, he claimed, were hungry. In Matanzas, a woman was wrapped in a Peruvian flag soaked in kerosene and set afire. At Ultimo Retiro, the boss and his henchmen blindfolded the indigenous girls and took them out to the patio to be shot. The head of this post, José Fonseca, was the greatest "reducer" of Indians in all of the Putumayo: one day he managed to round up several hundreds of Chontaduras, Ocana, and Utiguene Indians—men, women, and children—and launched a fusillade against them; one hundred and fifty Indians were slaughtered that day. In 1906, on Easter Sunday, he saw some Aifuga Indians coming to the well for water. "This is how we celebrate Easter around here," he said, and opened fire. A man and a fifteen-year-old girl were shot down. When he ordered raids against the Indians who were still free or who had escaped, he demanded that his men bring back the heads of their victims wrapped in a banana leaf....

The head of the garrison at Matanzas was a twenty-two-year-old blackguard named Armando Normand, who did not hesitate to order fifty lashes of the whip for a man suspected of stealing food. He also organized shooting matches with a disgustingly morbid object: to keep the target alive, but to shoot off his nose, ear, finger, penis, or testicle....

One common tactic of the rubber bosses: "Kill the parents to rape their daughters." Indian girls were taken from their villages and placed in brothels in rubber company centers. "The Convent School" was what the one in El Encanto was called; its "boarders" were between nine and fifteen years old. In this country, called "the devil's paradise" by a British newspaper, rapes were common currency; sometimes, no doubt to increase the enjoyment, the head of the family was locked in an iron collar so that he could watch the violation of his children.

In five years, according to the *Casement Report,* the Indian population in the region fell from fifty thousand to eight thousand and the forest became a vast charnel house ("battlefield strewn with bones"). As early as December 1907, an American consul suggested that if nothing were done to stop the carnage, the Indians would disappear within twenty years; the anthropologist William Curtis Farabee also denounced the feudal methods in the Putumayo valley.

After Casement's revelations, the toll continued to rise. The Peruvian government declared itself powerless to enforce the law in these inaccessible provinces. (Anyway, it condoned slavery of a very similar type in the Andes.) The rubber continued to flow to Manaos. In spite of the lawsuit brought by the shareholders of the company, if the world rubber market had not collapsed, it is quite likely that the ravage of the Putumayo valley would have continued unabated.

THE STORY OF ROSARIO DE CAMPOS, WIFE OF A BOLIVIAN RUBBER TAPPER

There are still rubber companies operating in the areas where the Indians were enslaved earlier in this century. Here is a story from one of them, a summary of the record of a trial in Riberalta:

M. Rafael Aponte took the stand to present his testimony concerning the disappearance of Rosario N. from the *Florida* rubber plantation....

Rosario was the wife of Luis Campos, a rubber tapper in one of the "centers" of the Florida plantation. One day, Samuel Castro, the production manager, was making a tour of inspection and noticed the young woman. Sometime later, he sent Campos on an exploratory canoe expedition in the Madre de Dios. Campos objected violently, insisting that this was not his job, but Castro was adamant, and Campos was forced to leave. While he was gone, Castro attempted to seduce his wife. Warned by a friend, Campos managed to return home, where Rosario confirmed that she had not been able to get rid of Castro, who had forced his attentions upon her. Castro was quickly informed of this untimely arrival, and the next day he called Campos into his office: Campos was given a vicious whipping and then packed off to another center. As for Rosario, she was forced to go live with "La Fortunata," a procuress in the pay of the administrator.

Two months later Rosario was Castro's mistress. But "La Fortunata" soon began to feel that she had not been paid generously enough for her services, and, in revenge, she managed to arrange for the young couple to meet. Castro caught them at it one day without their being aware they had been seen. The morning after, without saying a word to anyone, he led Rosario out on a walk. She had not returned by nightfall.

The next day, a rubber tapper came to tell Rafael Aponte that he had seen a dead body in the forest, a corpse tied to a palo santo tree—a tree with a soft center in which carnivorous ants nest—and he led Aponte to the macabre scene. It was a scene of inexpressible horror: a bloody skeleton was attached to the tree, tied to the trunk with hemp rope; little bits of flesh still clung to it here and there, crawling with thousands of ants. The two men discovered Rosario's torn clothes buried near the spot where she had been tortured. Castro had beaten the young woman, undressed her, and tied her to the stake, leaving her to the murderous insects.

The crimes of maniacs are not unusual in the jungle. It is very rare for the courts to get involved. After all, they are no match for the "powers that be." The Indian is the traditional scapegoat: white justice does not apply to him.

IT IS NOT A CRIME TO KILL AN INDIAN

The indigenous populations were continually mistreated by farmers, ranchers, gold seekers, diamond hunters. A complicit silence provided shameful protection. The accusations made by ethnologists and missionaries were not heard. It was not until quite recently with the eruption of a scandal implicating most of of the SPI officials that the truth of several accusations made at least thirty years ago was recognized. The Brazilian economy was experiencing a period of expansion in cacao production. The planters in the region of Bahia were colonizing the interior. To chase the Pataxos Indians from the territory they coveted, they did not hesitate to spread smallpox among them to kill them. The crime was denounced at the time, but there was a formal denial. The guilty parties, as a matter of fact, were among the political supporters of Juracy Magalhaes, the governor of the State, which is to say that they were untouchable. And it was only recently, in the course of an inquiry into the actions of the SPI, that an old inspector for the Service, Helio Jorge Bucker, confirmed the massacre of the Pataxos and gave the names of the criminals. When Hardenburg had tried to publicize what he saw in the Putumayo, one of his friends told him, "No one will believe us, especially if we tell the *whole* truth." Among the charges currently filed against the SPI (murder, torture, embezzlement, falsification of official documents), there is no mention of genocide. There is still reluctance to address the policy that the word implies. People can accept a murder, even a series of murders. And accidents, any crime. But to recognize the existence of a policy aimed at extermination? The international experts go along with this folly and play dumb. Why do sixty-seven million Brazilians feel the need to sacrifice a few tens of thousands of Indians in order to achieve national unity? Why does doña Edelmira Hoyos de Zarate, a wealthy Peruvian landowner in the province of Cajamarca, have to shoot seven peasants for using a small patch of land on her estate? Why do the prospectors for the International Petroleum Company have to turn their machine guns on the Anahuaca Indians in Madre de Dios?

In fact, as we have said, the story is as old as the New World: the Indian genocide began at the dawn of the conquest and has continued ever since; if there is anything surprising about it at all in our era, it is the fact that there are still a few survivors. For a long time the natives were protected by the hostility of their environment; but neo-colonialism developed technical resources that allowed it every sort of freedom; the Indians could not escape.

Why should they be spared, these people bereft of reason, these barefoot heretics? In Hispaniola, the Carib and Arawak Indians disappeared in less than a century. Pizarro in Peru, Cortés in Mexico used crime and torture without remorse. Gaspar de Carvajal, one of Orellana's companions, spoke indifferently of their treatment of the tribes encountered along the Amazon: "Our harquebuses got the better of the filthy people."

The first crimes were committed on the grounds of the state of war, which provided the arguments to justify the following sentiment: "The sword and the iron rod are the best instruments for the propagation of the faith," to quote the Jesuit Joseph de Anchieta. Henceforward, the extermination of the rebels became a military exploit, something to brag about. And there were plenty of braggarts. In 1664, Pedro da Costa Favella burned three hundred villages, killed eight hundred Indians, and enslaved four hundred others. One of his contemporaries, Captain Bento Maciel Parente boasted of having knocked off fifteen thousand Tapajoz Indians in a single day. In 1729, Belchior Mendes de Morais proudly told the governor of Belem that he had eliminated some twenty thousand eight hundred natives.

Treachery and the betrayal of confidence were the advance guard of civilization. The empire of the Incas, and that of the Aztecs, accepted the word of a white man and were conquered without a struggle. From that point on, relations between civilized and indigenous peoples were based on deception. In 1765, at the marquis de Pombal's command, the governor of Goias, Tristão da Cunha, succeeded in convincing the Xavantes to come and settle in the capital of the state. He soon regretted it, because his guests, who arrived by the thousands, quickly went through the provisions that were put at their disposal. Since he did not know what to do with these guests who had become a burden, he called out the Portuguese army to drive them away. A good half of the Xavantes died there; the others fled and developed the reputation of being savage, untamable "Indios bravos," a reputation that they have kept to this day. When Pimental Barbosa tried to get them to surrender to the SPI, his entire group was massacred; the Xavantes, it seems, had discovered some cases of guns and suspected a new trap.

Declaring the Indians to be "Indios bravos" (the adjective borrows a bull-fighting term: the bull is a *bravo;* the cows are *mansos*) simultaneously justifies any harsh treatment given to them and any measures taken against them in the aid or defense of "Indios mansos," the peaceful, semicivilized Indians who are supposedly threatened. Since there are good and bad Indians, it is up to the whites to determine their future.

The Xavantes, they claim, terrorize the neighboring tribes, especially the Tapirapé. It is only fair to protect them from danger.... Suddenly any measures taken against them become legitimate.

In the past few years, the Cintas Largas have developed a fierce reputation. Just recently, Colonel Hamilton de Castro, director of the SPI, received a report from Porto Velho listing their misdeeds: since 1965, they have stepped up their attacks against the rubber tappers who have already counted a dozen dead and many more wounded and who undoubtedly are preparing an answer to this violence. But do not forget that in August 1963 the boss of a rubber plantation launched an attack against the Cintas Largas in the area of Juina Mirim. A village there was completely razed. Afterward, the ethnologist Georg Grünberg was shown a photograph of a young Indian girl hung by her feet and disemboweled. As one reprisal led to another, the Cintas Largas acquired a reputation for terrifying savagery. On this basis their extermination has been justified. So they were recently given poisoned sugar. And an even more effective measure was taken: hired killers aboard small planes threw sticks of dynamite into the Indian camps, while their accomplices stood guard around the village to cut off the Indians' escape. Any free Indians, that is, any Indians who have not been subdued, receive the treatment of barbarians: at the end of the last century, the sheepherders in Tierra del Fuego and Patagonia paid up to a pound sterling for the left ear of an Indian; they were soon forced to insist on the whole head because so many men were cutting off an ear. Father Emilio Antonio Martinez recently traveled throughout Tierra del Fuego without seeing a single Indian: Ona, Yagan, and Alacalufe had all been exterminated.

In Paraguay, the Guayaki Indians have gradually been driven into smaller and smaller territories. To compensate for the resulting shortage of game, they conduct raids on the herds grazing around the "ranchos." This gives the ranchers an excuse for reprisal attacks on these cattle rustlers, who are surrounded by such horrible legends; so awful, they are not too far from the tales of the first chroniclers, who described the Indians as "diabolical creatures who eat human flesh and live coals." "It is not a crime to kill an Indian," a Paraguayan from San Juan de Nepomuceno told us. A Swiss man living in Paraguay told Jean Vellard this ghastly story: when he was on an expedition in the forest, one of his guides noticed a Guayaki Indian and shot him before our Swiss friend could stop him. As punishment, our friend sent him to the end of the convoy. Not having understood the reason for this treatment, the guide came back two days later with a present for his master, an unusual little pouch that he had made himself ... from the breast of his unfortunate victim.

Paul Rivet spoke out at the time against the actions of a group of "explorers" who took a grim toll in the frontier zones of Brazil and Paraguay. These men, armed with rifles and cameras, were professional Indian hunters who —and this fact stuns us—filmed the deaths of their victims. In the course of their campaigns, they slaughtered Guayaki in Paraguay, Tupi-Guarani in Brazil, and Matako in the Argentine Chaco. To avoid the tiresome delay that would result if customs agents got too curious, they carried medicine and, especially, craniometers, to establish the scientific nature of their project. Thus, they could embark on their criminal tours with confidence.

In Brazil, a *fazendeiro* from Gaiaba liked to hang Indian girls by the feet and cut them up with a cleaver. Justice, here like everywhere else, did not even make a pretense of interfering with this practice.

There was—as we have already said—a *myth of the bad Indian.* All the stories describing the violent acts that the Indians were supposed to have committed created such a climate of fear that the most peaceful party of Indians could inspire terror: in the Upper Orinoco, a North American explorer, Hamilton Rice, was forced to stop his team on the edge of a river so that his cargo could be transported across a rapid. Some Guaharibo Indians came up, talking and gesturing, without any sign of hostility. But Mr. Rice had been so impressed by the tales of his guide, that he panicked and ordered his men to shoot....

The Villas-Boas brothers tell a similar story about the Kayapo Indians: one day a large group of them appeared at the military base in Cachimbo. The pilots flew into a panic and fired at them with antiaircraft guns; some of the pilots even leapt into their planes, took off, and flew over the Indians at low altitudes, shooting at them. Why the massacre? How can their panic be explained? These aviators had been trading with the Indians for a long time, exchanging store-bought trinkets for feather ornaments, which they resold to foreign museums and to gift shops in the big cities.

The punishments do not seem to fit the crimes: in 1956, the administrators of the Alto-Tapajos Company organized a retaliatory raid against the Kayapo who had stolen flour and a few worthless objects from an abandoned warehouse. Twenty Indians were murdered while they slept. Their murderers, who had political support, were never even bothered.

The national authorities, in closing their eyes to these criminal actions, are actually encouraging them in order to rid themselves of a problem that they seem incabable of solving. An episode from the colonization of Argentina illustrates this:

At the end of the last century, European colonists settling in the province of Santa-Fé, in northern Argentina, took it upon themselves to eliminate the Indians who stood in the way of their plans for expansion. One of them, Teofilo Romang, told this story: being taken for a doctor by a cacique who was sick, he had poisoned the chief while pretending to give him medicine. In a legitimate response to this sort of action the Indians launched attacks against the young colonies. But in doing so they laid themselves open to the most savage repression. In 1875, Romang and a North American from the region, Guillermo Moore, organized the men and led a series of raids against the indigenous camps in the area. In a report that they made to the authorities of the province, the colonists described their exploits this way: "It was barely daybreak when we began firing; within minutes, our efforts were rewarded with a complete victory. The bodies of twenty-nine dead Indians were strewn about the camp and another twenty lay wounded." A little later, "At dawn we approached a camp without being discovered. A woman ran from her rancho and gave a scream; it was her last. Then the men tried to flee through the underbrush. But we fired upon them quickly enough to kill a few of them and wound many others." As a result of this butchery, in which no death toll was ever established, the Indians took refuge in military bases and missions to escape expeditions, the avowed purpose of which was "to kill and capture Indians." As for the provincial authorities, they did not even consider using sanctions; they were overjoyed that the colonists were taking charge of ""resolving" the delicate problem of their relationship with the savages of the region.

According to Father Martinez, director of the Agency for Indigenous Affairs, there are one hundred and fifty thousand Indians left in Argentina, or about .6% of the total population; this allows the government to claim that there is no Indian problem in their country and to ignore the groups of Indians struggling to survive and abandon them to their misery, to disease and hunger. An official report stated, "Whoever has witnessed the horrible sight of a group of aborigines (women, children, and the elderly) fighting like a pack of dogs in the dust on the tracks for the few scraps of bread that travelers have thrown from their railroad cars, can only blush at the thought that this occurs in our country." We ourselves have witnessed similar scenes in the Andes and the Rio Plata region.

DISEASE IN THE SERVICE OF THE COLONISTS

As we have said, disease takes a terrible toll on the Indians, who lack immunity and health care. The statistics are painfully eloquent: in the nineteenth century, the Munduruku, who had numbered nearly nineteen thousand, were reduced to a mere twelve hundred; the Nambikwara went from ten thousand to one thousand; the Kaingang of the state of São Paulo, from twelve hundred to eighty-seven. In one day, the Xocren of the state of Santa Catarina went from eight hundred to one hundred and eighty-nine. The Kayapo of the region of Conceição de l'Araguaya, in northern Brazil, numbered five or six thousand in 1900, when the first missionaries arrived; by 1922, they had already been reduced to five or six hundred; in 1929, following an outbreak of influenza, there were only about fifty left, and these were then reduced further by bronchopneumonia and measles. The flu that ravaged Europe at the end of the First World War also attacked the Guayaki of Paraguay.

The first missionaries were not surprised at the vulnerability of the natives to diseases that were relatively mild among Europeans. They saw it as punishment from heaven exacted upon the pagans who refused to listen to the Evangelists; the catechists often expressed this belief in their writings: "And to chastise them, they were struck by a plague that decimated them."

There is only a small step between observing this weakness and exploiting it, and that step was quickly taken. In 1710, the English distributed "peace offerings" to the Canadian Indians, the Abenaki, the Micmac, and the Etchémi, blankets contaminated with smallpox. In Peru, the colonists in Ucayali gave the Campa Indians bolts of infected fabric. The same method was used to decimate the Pataxos of the Brazilian state of Bahia.

Sometimes the colonists did not even have to take action, since epidemics occurred naturally; during the summer of 1933, the Toba-Pilaga of the Gran Chaco were decimated by an outbreak of chickenpox. The soldiers stationed in the forts in the region certainly did not to come to their aid, since, in the words of a *poblador* of the time, the Indians' death was seen as a veritable "New Year's gift." Just as criminal was the negligence of the Brazilian SPI, which did not take the most basic health precautions. Their guilt goes even farther: since they did not budget enough money to provide regular medical service, the pacified Indians were virtually doomed. Again in 1955 they let the Kayapo die without coming to their aid when epidemics struck.

Poisoned gifts were part of the white man's toolkit. In 1860, some Apaches were invited to a carefully prepared banquet from which they never returned. When Nicolas Suarez wanted to exploit the forest of Acre, he saw the Indians as no more than a nuisance; several casks of poisoned alcohol were left on the river banks. Occasionally he also left clothes on the edge of the village, clothes that had been worn by someone ill with measles.

Arsenic mixed with sugar was the method used to eliminate the Cintas Largas and the Tapaiauna. In 1960, poisoned rice, ostensibly a gift for the Beiços of Pau, was left along the left bank of the middle fork of the Arinas River, but, fortunately, the Indians did not realize that it was a gift intended for them....

SETTLERS VERSUS INDIANS

As the settled zone grew, the Indians' territory continued to shrink until they had no choice but to disappear. In the state of São Paulo, the coffee plantations have pushed back the forest; waves of settlers, cattle ranchers and farmers, are now advancing on the Mato Grosso. With each "cycle of exploitation," sugar, coffee, cacao, the Indians are forced to give up their territory. In the early part of this century, the Germans in the São Paulo region complained that the indigenous peoples did not provide an effective work force and were actually a liability; the Germans had guns and few scruples: the Indians did not last long.

Cattle ranchers have ravaged the entire continent: destroying the autochthonous groups in Patagonia; persecuting and enslaving the Guayaki in Paraguay; completely eliminating the Charrua in Uruguay.... In 1930, a Brazilian ethnologist went searching for the Oti Indians, who live southeast of São Paulo, near the Paranapanema river.... There were only two women and one child left: when the settlers arrived with their cattle, the Oti—who had been deprived of their traditional resources by the whites' hunting— had treated the cows like prize game. The settlers used this as a pretext for harassing and hounding them until they were eliminated. Two sayings sum up the attitude of the big cattle ranchers: "Cattle and Indians don't mix" and "See an Indian, kill an Indian."

Once the settlers arrive, the game disappears: experts state that in a twenty-year period, their uncontrolled hunting completely emptied the forest of tapirs and deer. Fish are also becoming scarce; life in the rivers has been destroyed by fishing with dynamite. The tortoises are disappearing and the lamantin already have. If famine has always occurred periodically in the Amazon, it has become chronic since the white man settled there and began his depredation.

CHRONICLE OF THE SPI; OR, A STORY OF FAILURE

When General Rondon created the SPI, he believed he would be able to stand up to the speculators and oppose their projects. But it was difficult for him to prevail against economic and political interests. At least he made an effort to obtain territory for the tribes that were pacified, even when he was forced to move them to satisfy the demands of the settlers. In 1938, the main Kraho village was surrounded by workers employed by the area's two largest ranchers, who had decided to take advantage of the fact that the men were away hunting. Sixty tribe members, all women and children, were killed. Rondon learned of this and managed to obtain the cooperation of the army, who arrested the two men responsible. They were tried and the criminals were sentenced to eight years in prison.

The settlers were insatiable, and the power of the SPI became increasingly restricted. In 1940, General Rondon was ousted and, after that, the agency rarely intervened in defense of the people it was supposed to be protecting. The officials who were most active were gradually forced out and replaced by men who were less principled and easier to corrupt.

Fazendeiros and rubber workers terrorized these defenseless Indian populations any way they liked. A Brazilian journalist wrote in *O Globo* that "one of the methods employed by the criminals consists of cutting the Indian in two with an ax if he objects to abandoning his land."

The *garimpeiros,* prospectors for gold and diamonds, have taken over the river banks, devastating them. Nothing matters to garimpeiros but the gold nuggets or the strike they imagine they will find someday. Any intruders on their claim are shot in the back: prospectors denied a Bororo tribe access to the stream near their camp, not even allowing them to drink from it.... In their murderous folly, they almost exterminated a tribe of Chicon Indians; the Villas-Boas brothers found fifty-four survivors *in extremis* and were able to save them, moving them to the Xingu National Park.

A new scourge is threatening the Brazilian Amazon: the *grilheiros,* or land speculators. These men dispute the Indians' right to the lands that were assigned to them by Rondon; they have been trying to sell them since 1958. Two deputies in Mato Grosso decided that the Kaduveo territory belonged to the state, and that therefore the state could decide to sell it, which they did in 1960, earning a substantial profit. In 1959, the government of the State of Goias decreed that the Island of Bananal, where the Karaja had settled, did not fall under the jurisdiction of the maritime department, that Goias controlled it and could sell it. Complaints were addressed to the deputy chief of the SPI, who maintained that all necessary measures had been taken, a statement that was later disproved. At the time of the purchase, two prices were offered: one for the land with the Indians on it; another, much higher, if the property was cleared. Here is the usual technique for clearing Indian land: first, a small tourist plane flies a reconnaissance mission to locate the Indian villages; then a force of about fifty men is sent in; the men launch a surprise attack, surrounding a village and using hand-held machine guns to empty it out. The army secretly provides the murderers with these hand-held weapons, which are small and easy to handle. Everyone in Brazil knows how these *piripiri* are used.

In 1948, Nimuendaju had warned the SPI that there was an attack planned against the Tikuna of Upper Solimoes; he was even able to obtain some of the adventurers' grenades, which he used to corroborate his accusation. So the Tikuna were saved. But it was only a reprieve. In the frontier zones of Colombia and Brazil, they have become the victims of rubber company workers, traffickers in every sort of commodity, and smugglers, who give them alcohol and guns and purchase their services, eventually setting them against one another as hired men for rival gangs. At the present time there is an outbreak of leprosy among them and they are rotting away; rather than provide aid, the government simply exiles them to the island of Armaça or Araria where they die a painful death. Leprosy is no longer an incurable disease and there are treatment facilities in Brazil; but why should the government care for people if it has no idea what to do with them?

On the border between Venezuela and Colombia, the Indians often end up paying for the smuggling that occurs in the region. Doctor Pierre Couret reported a recent "incident" that occurred in the state of Apure at the beginning of 1968. The overseer of an estate had invited some Indian workers to a party given at a Colombian development site near the border. On the day of the party, the Indians arrived with their families. But while the drinking was going on, the women were raped, and a massacre ensued. Sixteen Indians, including women and children, were tortured and executed; some of them were tied to horses and dragged along the ground. Drunken violence? Perhaps.... But it is more likely that it was a premeditated action, intended to eliminate the witnesses to various illegal activities. No one would ever have known anything about it if two Indians had not managed to escape the bloodbath; they went to the estate owner Marcelo T. and told him what had happened. He accompanied them to Caracas where they filed a complaint. In typical Western fashion, people in the capital reacted with outrage; the inhabitants of the State of Apure wondered why there was so much fuss about such an ordinary occurrence....

In Brazil, the SPI has gone from negligence of the Indians' interests to a criminal complicity with their enemies. The low salaries paid by the government may provide a partial explanation for the unforgivable venality of the officials. The most scandalous stories are heard, but when humanitarian protests are made, they get lost in a maze of bureaucracy. The violence and brutality go unpunished. Some examples?

Flavio Abreu, an official of the Seventh Regional Office of the SPI (Rio Grande do Sul, Parana, Santa Catarina) traded an eleven-year-old Indian girl for a clay oven.

The SPI served the Cintas Largas of the State of Para a meal liberally seasoned with arsenic.

The wife of an SPI agent forced a Cintas Largas woman to spend the night standing in a pit because her husband did not want to work as a slave....

Ramis Bucair, an official of the SPI, told the *Jornal do Brasil* that in December 1967 several Nambikwara were killed by machine-gun fire near Vila-Bela (in the state of Mato Grosso).

On the night of 21–22 October 1966, the Guajajara Indians in the town of Guaruru (state of Maranon) were attacked by some whites from the village of Campo Formosa. It was a vigilante raid to punish an Indian who had refused to surrender his horse to a white without compensation. No action was taken against the two whites involved, Firminio Sales and Antonio Dantas, a candidate for the deputyship, since they were leading citizens.

An investigation of the SPI followed. Of seven hundred employees, one hundred and thirty-four were charged, two hundred were fired. It is estimated that within a fifteen-year period, eighteen thousand forest Indians perished in Brazil. Twenty million dollars were embezzled; some of the money taken was earmarked to provide schools and hospitals; consequently, these were never built. The food and supplies that were intended for the Indians reappeared for sale in the markets. As for the goods that the whites bought from Indians—wood, skins, food they had harvested, and handicraft items—the Indians were paid a pathetically low price.

Major Luis Vinhas Neves, ex-director of the SPI, was indicted; he was charged with forty-two crimes; Judge Kader Figueirero, presiding over the trial, declared that the defendant had embezzled more than three hundred thousand dollars in two years.... And this was the same Vinhas Neves who claimed he was trying to give the Indians a national consciousness by drafting them into the military service and making them work so that they would be solvent: "The Indians are irresponsible children.... By working they will become adults and become part of the national community," he had stated. He had then provided a personal demonstration of what a civilized white adult means by national community. "There is no crime that Neves has not committed, from robbery to rape, from the theft of lands to the assassination of men, from torture to prostitution," declared Judge Figueirero.

The Brazilian joke goes that SPI actually stands for "Service for the Prostitution of the Indian." People act indignant; they denounce the abuses. Yet in Amazonia the massacres continue. In the Maranon, Japanese ranchers have hired killers to eliminate the Beiços of Pau. In Brasilia, the Ministry of Agriculture, which housed the archives of the SPI was destroyed in a fire— it was too convenient for it to have been an accident....

One cannot help suspecting that the scandal has been covered up for political reasons and that the decisions by the courts in the capital have no effect on the agony of the sixty thousand Indians who remain in the Brazilian Amazon. After gold, diamonds, and rubber, now it is uranium and manganese that prospectors are seeking in the forest.

The Indians seem more and more anachronistic. They stand in the way of the advance of progress. As we have said, there is only a tiny distinction between letting them die and murdering them. In either case, they are denied the right to life. Paul Lambert tells this story: in 1963, he was invited to Manaos to go on a "safari," with a fairly unsavory objective; his companions were going to destroy an Indian village; they described—in all innocence—the fun they would have on the expedition: "We throw babies into the air and catch them when they come down on bush knives. Afterwards, we clean out the village with grenades. We get paid for each pair of ears."

There have been a few efforts to ensure the Indians their freedom and dignity: in 1958, Father Emilio Antonio Martinez went to Geneva to attend a meeting of the International Office on Indian Affairs to demand that the Andean Plan, whose purpose is to improve the conditions of the Indians in Peru, Ecuador, and Bolivia, be extended to include Argentina. But the official representative from Argentina objected, pointing out that Argentina does not have an Indian problem....

In 1961, Dr. Harald Schultz was in the United States and was able to meet with the UN official in charge of racial minorities; he was informed that to initiate an action, the UN must be presented with a complaint from a foreign government, not from a single individual.

Alfred Métraux has repeatedly denounced a government policy of pacification that has become synonymous with destruction. The SPI has betrayed its goals and become a weapon wielded by whites; it no longer works to preserve the savagery of the Indians and their traditional way of life but aims isntead to integrate them into modern society as quickly as possible, at any cost. In 1944, several rubber workers ambushed some Kukraïmoro Indians from Xingu. Nine Indians were killed and the rest of the tribe retreated deep into the forest. The SPI managed to "pacify" them in 1947. What sort of peace was offered to them? One hundred and seventeen of them were transported to a Xingu island that had neither hunting grounds nor tillable fields. In less than a year, half of the group had succumbed to diseases they contracted from contact with the neo-Brazilians who passed through their village.... Métraux thought that the creation of preserves where the Indians would be protected might well be a positive development.

In 1901, President Janio Cuadros bowed to demands made by the Villas-Boas brothers and signed a bill authorizing the establishment of a preserve, the Xingu National Park. This territory, nearly twenty-five-thousand square miles, a fairly healthy area, was placed under the control of the University of Brasilia and its management was entrusted to the Villas-Boas brothers. Access to it is difficult and, at least theoretically, is forbidden to whites (still, three-quarters of the articles devoted to "the people we call savages" come from the park). About eighteen hundred Indians from fifteen tribes have been gathered there, and a special effort has been made to relocate the Indians who are most directly threatened by extermination. The Villas-Boas brothers thought that the establishment of a reservation would enable them to familiarize their protégés with the Western world gradually and also to convince the whites that the Indians are human and that Brazilian society has an obligation to them.

It is legitimate to question whether a reservation is a real solution; it is so controlled and so shielded from the outside. Groups that have already been hunted and partially destroyed have taken refuge there, as if the reservation provides them a brief respite before the inevitable end. And although there has been a tremendous effort to preserve the tribes that are on their way to disappearing, there is no way to stop the massacres that are still occurring. In January 1966, the Jesuit priest Waldemar Weber made the following statement to the *Jornal do Brasil*: "Some whites were traveling through the region of Xingu-Tapajos to exterminate seven thousand Indians there. The Indians who were chased from their villages were hunted down and shot with rifles or killed by machine-gun fire and grenades."

In 1967, the SPI was incorporated into a more general organization, the National Foundation for the Indian. The council director was given the following mandates: to represent Indian interests and provide the legal assistance necessary to protect Indian rights; and to uphold respect for the person of the Indian, his institutions, and tribal communities.

Will this council have any real power, and will its decisions have any real impact? After all, since the nineteenth century, there have been many efforts to define the status of Indians in order to help and protect them.

LAW AND THE INDIAN

When Latin America gained independence and formed separate countries, the grand principles of the French revolution were raised as standards. All men would be equal before the law. This high-minded principle meant that the Indians were subject to even more rigorous constraint, because until this time the statute of exception had provided a certain amount of protection for them. In the Andes, the rules of private property freed the Indian to dispose of his land—he could sell or exchange it—and did not stop whites from ruining the unfortunate Indian who did not understand the contracts he was forced to sign. Once he was a citizen, the Indian was drafted into military service; recruiting agents came to drag him away from his family, who were left devastated by this incomprehensible turn of events. Recognition of the Indians' legal equality only served to sustain their actual inequality, even to increase it, since the liberation of the South American republics from Europe did not bring about a change in the internal structures of the countries, nor did it bring about the end of colonialism.

A few responsible voices were raised. There were movements to safeguard the Indians, sometimes taking the form of political movements with lists of demands. During the entire nineteenth century, as in earlier centuries, the Indians were under the protection of the Church; today, the state has taken charge of the indigenous populations. Most of the Indian laws, enacted at the beginning of the twentieth century, treat the Indian as a minor, who must be kept under guardianship until he matures sufficiently to be integrated into national society.

The Brazilian code of 1916 treated the Indian as entirely irresponsible; the 1942 law accorded him some responsibility, comparable to that of a minor or a married woman. In Paraguay, Indians are exempt from prosecution, like juveniles.... This is probably the reason they are treated indulgently when they enter the courts; but isn't the way they are treated a denial of their right to existence by the whites in power?

In 1940, at the Inter-American Indigenist Congress in Patzcuaro, it was decided to recognize the autonomy of indigenous groups as well as their right to preserve their organization, an organization founded on a specific heritage of customs and traditions. After this statement, a lot of "indigenist institutes" were created, but they do not have the power or the financial resources to accomplish any effective action. Between the projects envisioned by people with good intentions and the completion of those projects is erected the barrier of a utilitarian and mercantile West.

Because of the poverty of these national organizations, a few leaders, such as Harald Schultz and Father Martinez, have made pleas to the international community. But they have been caught in the snares of diplomacy and have been unable to avoid raising new problems that they are unable to solve.

Following a scandal that shook Brazil, a number of protests were sent to President Castelo Branco; several university associations drafted manifestos and set up information campaigns.*

In September 1968, the Commission of International Jurists stated that a "true genocide" is presently occurring in Brazil. This is "genocide in the strictest sense of the term," as defined among the three categories of crimes covered by Article 6 of the Nuremberg statute. The international convention of 9 December 1948 established this definition: "Genocide consists of the destruction or persecution of human groups that are conceived as national, ethnic, racial, or religious entities."

When we ignore the plight of several thousand Indians condemned in the name of supposed economic progress and a false theory of evolution, we make the implicit confession that human life is not worth very much in our civilized world.

SAVE THE INDIAN

At the most fundamental level, the history of thought about primitive people—are they human, overgrown children, or replicas of early stages of Western civilization?—provides a summary of the changes that have taken place in our own culture: the West knows that it can no longer hold exclu-

---

* Notably the Society of Americanists, which on 3 July 1968 decided to form a commission to safeguard the Indians. Mr. Robert Jaulin is one of the principal leaders of this commission.

sive power, but it still considers itself the dominant power. Western ignorance follows from this error. Our taste for exoticism and our morality stem from it, as does the deadly intolerance that seems lodged in our hearts. Centuries of culture and well-intentioned unreasonableness, centuries of humanism have led to the most heinous of all crimes: genocide.

Entire communities forced to abandon their lands, children kidnapped, people treated barbarously, degraded mentally and physically, punitive expeditions launched against them.... With genocide, with racism, we confront horror itself. We have spoken of the fragility of traditional societies, of the blind intolerance of our civilization toward the Indians, of the lack of understanding that has led the Amazonians—white, creole, and mestizo—to the organized extermination of the Indians. But there is one question that haunts us, that emerges through the pages of this case like the recurring notes of a flute, forcing us to weigh an unpleasant possibility. aren't we just as guilty of exploiting the Indians, aren't we indulging in a lot of useless discussion? But when we use the word *genocide*, we have no intention of turning ourselves into defenders of a lost cause; we do not see our roles as charity and moralism. We are not writing off the Indians; we do not believe that genocide should be considered an inevitable calamity.

Ethnographers must organize; they must enact plans to safeguard the threatened minorities—this is important. But if they do not capture public opinion, their projects will not produce results. More than anything, ethnographers need to launch an information campaign, a sound and systematic campaign. The general public has the right to know. The right and the duty. To accept this atrocity, to allow these terrible crimes to be committed, is to become an accomplice in them.

Do not misjudge us: our indignation is not mere posturing. We are convinced that it is possible to affect the policy of Latin American governments. Especially since these countries, while dependent on the United States economically, still turn toward Europe culturally. We can say to them without paternalism: the sense Latin Americans have of their countries still comes from Europe. Why shouldn't they learn a respect for their indigenous populations from Europe, just as they have acquired a taste for pre-Colombian antiquities and folklore? In our view, the salvation of the Indian must begin here and now....

PART THREE

Song of Silbaco

NOTES

FROM

A

TRIP

WE DO NOT SEEK THE sunny vacuity of vacations, nor to travel with the crowd. Better to journey over endless plains, cross deserts, struggle through this infernal congregation of trees. And so become vandals entering this, the most Gothic of forests! ... We don't want artistic effects, half-tones, oh, a chaste shade lowered the better to trifle with one's passions and betray one's memories! We can tolerate only frank darkness or full sunlight. Silence. Thirty-six thousand sky-blue pitchers, petrels in the air. As for the forest, we prefer it vast and ancestral. And no matter how thick the forest, we are not afraid, and we will not be lost.

—J. M.

T

O TRAVEL IS TO REFUSE to sit and think. A new form of skepticism? All in all, I would let Jean-Jacques Rousseau have the last word: "The knowledge obtained from one's travel corresponds to the purpose with which it is undertaken."

We are anchored at Guayaramerin, a small port on the border between Brazil and Bolivia; its warm climate has slowed us down. Stretched out in my hammock, smoking a pipe filled with native tobacco, I feel the rhythm of rivers flowing to the sea. I drink *chicha;* fresh and sweet at first, this corn beer leaves a taste of yeast in my mouth. My cabin is packed with reassuring objects: mosquito netting, maps and compasses, medical supplies, camera equipment, trade goods, a rifle and ammunition. As a traveler, I take the middle road between bourgeois and adventurer.

Jacques Chabert and I have been waiting more than a week on the boat that is supposed to take us to Puerto Chacobo. Our guides have been trying in vain to buy fuel. We took advantage of the wait to tend to odds and ends, to mend and fill the holes enlarged by five months of wandering. Then we had to think about our plan for the exploration of Upper Yata, the swampy area draining into the Amazon basin, the territory of the Chacobo Indians. Would a little rice, some noodles, some sugar, and a few liters of oil be enough to allay our hunger? That is a question worth pondering; we juggle calories and pounds of noodles. Finally, we agree on some figures—they are completely unreasonable.

We are a long way from the sensual intimacy of the jungle. Guayaramerin, with its colonial architecture, constructed of gaudily painted adobe and tin roofs, seems to have only a provisional existence. The activity around the port splits into multiple scenes, multiple planes—each with a marvelous independence, interdependence. For sale, dirt-cheap, are animal skins, ocelot and cayman, bundles of rubber, Brazil nuts, cocaine. Bike-taxis shuttle between the riverfront station, a porticoed building covered with roman tiles, and Hernan-Roca-Casanova Plaza.... This is not the first time I have found myself in the middle of nowhere, without any money. Once again I will find myself registering the silence, the changing colors, of such a landscape, verifying the uniqueness of a small native tribe, wearing myself out to set down their customs, invoking the contrasts of exoticism.

I feel that I track the picturesque but, in my net of notes, capture only a caricature.

Nothing is simple. Today, before beginning a description that will necessarily be poor and naïve, I find myself assailed by those images that time has etched more sharply. One enters—good-bye, settlement zone!—dark walls of Amazonian forest, a long corridor of green where disorder and beauty reign. One feels very much an intruder, with the intruder's rage at the world being revealed, this world that is lost to view, outside oneself. The forest is inhabited by cruel spirits, deaf to sorrow and cries of protest. Everything that stings, everything that scratches, everything that bites. Plants and animals. Here men don't talk about them: they suffer, and they die.

The Chacobo Indians occupy a vast territory stretching between the Yvon and the Yata rivers. They rarely travel any distance from the banks of these sinuous streams, whose muddy waters carry flotsam, floating islands, and carrion. Hunters and seminomadic farmers, they take advantage of the dry season to explore their domain, to take an inventory of its resources.

The Indians of Upper Yata, with whom we lived for three months, form a subtribe of thirty-four individuals (five men, seven women, two adolescents, one young girl, and nineteen infants). Their permanent village stands on a rise that overlooks a lagoon; their huts are not grouped together but are linked by a path that runs alongside the river, and each of them has access to the water. It is impossible to think that this choice of location was determined by no more than necessity, or a vagary of fate. In fact, for all its isolation, it is crossed by footpaths going in all directions, hunting trails, so that one may leave the village from one end and reenter it at the other. The area of their activities, limited as it is, seems a topographic summary of eastern Bolivia: a chain of lakes, rivers, streams, forest clearings, scrub, savannahs.... The Chacobo Indians lack the sense of closure.

Stagnant water and submerged trees. A lagoon, some huts dried out by the sun. Under ramshackle roofs five fires are smouldering and there is smoke rising over the tops of the trees. The setting becomes familiar very quickly. My hammock and pipe reclaim me.

Meeting with the Indians. It's like a mail-order marriage. You know what they're like from photos, articles. Awkward motions, advance and retreat, trust and mistrust—how shall we approach them?

Our first contacts here were easy and friendly from the very beginning. The cacique—a man about forty years old—came over to us and without any ceremony, using sketchy gestures, invited our little group to drink some chicha and eat some roast monkey and tapir. The gourd passed from hand to hand. It would soon have been empty, but for one thing, they kept refilling it before handing it on to the next person. This had gone on for a long time, we knew our own limits and, after six gourds, we were able to appreciate those of the natives. I write this without boasting: theirs were inferior to those of the average Frenchman. One of our guides, feeling the effects of the liquor, tried to kill a scrawny chicken, but could not ruin this first exotic rendezvous.

As the numbness of night descended, the Chacobo revived the fire. Although it was not very cold, we were chilled and our stomachs uneasy. Here are the men: Kako, Kuya, Nako, Naro, Étachi. We shared a chunk of smoked meat. At this hour, when the moon had gone down and the sun was not yet up, Lucero—the star of hunters and rubber tappers—was alone in a sky that seemed sad and ordinary. Some parrots flew by in pairs.

We observed them and they observed us. I tried to pick out a theme, to define a style, but my thoughts always became tangled. What can I say about these men? Short, with dark, copper-colored skin; each has a pierced nose with crossed red feathers through the septum; each has two pointy cabay (capybara among the Guarani) teeth dangling from the lobes of his ears, which frame a strong and unlined face. They wear clothes made from plants, of hammered pith, and bracelets of bark. The women, with long jet-black hair, are pleasant looking, even pretty. No accretion of details can locate the center—the sense—of their archaic life; they do not even produce an accurate and lifelike sketch. We must choose the point of view, the illumination.

A glimmer of a thought: not too long ago ethnologists would have tried to place these societies within the chorus of nations. Of course, this needed to be qualified: savage societies, primitive societies, societies without writing, exotic societies.... We are well aware of the importance of such research. Today, however, it is appropriate to situate these groups within a political context. We describe them best by reducing them to a category that is both ambiguous and relative: marginal peoples.

These peoples—the Chacobo in particular—are the product of a long cultural agony. In fact, from 1780 to the end of the twentieth century, lowland Bolivia attracted adventurers of every sort who boasted of the advantages of Western civilization as they proposed "the domestication of the savages." And imposed it by violence, even going as far as leaving cases of poisoned liquor on the beaches; Law 44 prevailed. The Indians lost their customs and their beliefs, the more hostile among them took refuge in the depths of the jungle where they perished at the end of an adventure we cannot begin to comprehend. Their conquerors, marrying and establishing households, settled down and formed a colonial society. Thus, while indigenous cultures were disintegrating, a new regime was being created and there was no longer much talk of our "barbarity." A few humanists attempted to reestablish native cultures, without success; a few missionaries worked some wonders to wrest Indian souls from paganism. Nothing helped. They had lost the will to live.

By 1968, these peoples had been doubly forgotten. Without particular interests, travelers—whether specialists or not—were indifferent or cool toward them; Bolivian society did not recognize their culture. They survive on the fringes of the modern world.

The Indians of the Upper Yata are able to take what they find on the edge and improvise with it. They do a fair job of solving the practical problems of daily life but, being unable to perpetuate their tradition, they borrow or imitate the solutions of their conquerors. They scavenge and patch together. "On this trip," writes Claude Lévi-Strauss, "we are confronted by our whole unfortunate history." A story illustrates this point.

As I was writing in my notebook, the women and children came over and formed a circle around me. They stared curiously at the pages covered with graffiti. Nako tried to reproduce the marks; he worked for a moment and then, obviously frustrated, ripped out the page, crumpling it and crushing it under his foot.

He wept quietly.... The hill had become a vague landscape, the air smelled of decaying matter and dead water. While the women ground the corn in a flat mortar, I tried to record the mean—anachronistic—details of this savage life. The baskets suspended from the low beams of the hut's framework held a good many empty bottles, jars of jam, and parts of manufactured goods. The indigenous person, hobo-tinker, has an acute sense of the unwonted and is always fascinated by the technical "crafts" of our civilization.

The dogs howl and before the women lift their pestles from their work, the men return loaded down with game. They set their prey down in front of the fire and go stretch out in hammocks—the only Chacobo furniture—under which the children have scattered embers. Smoked, but protected from mosquitoes, the hunter rests. He removes his clothes and waits for the women to come and delouse him. That night, in a silence cut by ringing laughter, he will tell his family the tale of how the "manechi" monkeys had gotten away from him, and how, with a sharp eye and innumerable ruses, he had finally managed to attract them, imitating their cries. If you asked him in what part of the forest he had found them, he would indicate the mass of huge trees and say, "Over there."

The Chacobo Indians were not always jungle dwellers. Long ago, they were scattered between the Mamoré River and Lake Rogoaguado. Their wars against the Sinabo caused them to move to the north, where they eventually settled. Accustomed to living on the savannahs, they had to become acclimated, had to learn to take advantage of this singularly rich flora. Bananas were spread throughout South America in the seventeenth century and the Chacobo learned about them from other tribes, after which they became one of the staple crops they cultivated. They also grew corn, manioc, and pineapples. From the end of July until October, the women gathered wild berries and collected plants with healing properties. They had few domestic animals: dogs, monkeys, parrots (Ara), peccaries, musk ducks, and turkey cocks. On this subject, Paul Rivet notes: "The small number of domestic animals the Indians possess should be attributed more to the poverty of American fauna than to any failing on their part." The scarcity of foodstuffs has given them a certain wisdom: today they are able to take care of their needs.

To the Chacobo woman falls the task of wood gathering—which is difficult for her since pregnancy is her chronic state—as well as the important job of tending the fire and keeping the coals alive. During the long marches through the forest, she carries a hamper—holding it with a bark strap around her forehead—and a taper of glowing wood; the man walks in front with his bow and arrows. Here the woman fills the role of wife and mother; man is the hunter. He interprets jungle sounds and the cries of animals. He leaps into thickets, whistles, holds his breath, whistles again, and shoots off an arrow. He knows how to be cruel and how to kill with his bare hands when he finds a monkey wounded, hanging by its tail, suffering.

The Chacobo Indians like to compare themselves to different types of talking birds, *tojos* or *aymaristos,* which have the remarkable ability to imitate the song or cry of every animal, the ideal of all the young people. The tribe has no ceremony to mark the initiation of adolescents, but the careful observer would note that anyone who aspires to marriage, or who insists on speaking at tribal reunions, must necessarily be a proven hunter. There is only one way to gain proprietary rights in interfamilial affairs: to kill a tapir. The tapir, a quadruped having a short trunk-shaped nose and weighing as much—in this part of South America—as two hundred kilos, lives in the jungle clearings around swamplands and marshes. It is a timid animal with a ponderous gait and it does not let men get close to it. It makes tiny noises, almost exactly like those of a very common bird of prey called the *chuvi.* When the chuvi calls, the tapir answers and they approach each other: the chuvi comes and perches on the tapir, ridding it of the parasitic insects that devour its back. The Chacobo exploit this friendship between two such different animals. They imitate the call of the chuvi; the tapir answers and comes within range of their arrows. The first shot must pierce the neck, but quite often it's not enough to finish off such a large beast.... Étachi followed a wounded animal like this for an entire day; he returned to camp with a serious wound and several broken arrows; he told the men where his prey was lying. The others attacked the tapir in the middle of the night; they were drunk and chanting.

To be a man and survive, the Chacobo must prove himself again and again throughout his entire earthly sojourn. To kill a tapir is not enough. He must love his wife, feed his children, and maintain his household.

The following week we had the opportunity to participate in the construction of a large dwelling, a room without walls, roofed with *motacu* palms. It was interesting to see how this building, forty-five by thirty feet, was constructed. It all started on a note of comedy: Maro had tried to hang his hammock from two worm-eaten crossbars, and had pulled a part of the frame down onto his head. This fiasco made him furious and he swore, it seemed to me, like a real fiend. The tribal council met the same day and decided to rebuild. They would construct an identical hut. It had to respect the ancient orientation—perpendicular to the course of the sun—no variation would be tolerated. One team of workers demolished the old structure while another put up the new, copied so well that the new hut—built in five days—could have been mistaken for the one it replaced. This scrupulous respect for the architectural tradition was explained to me by Kuya. It revealed their wish to avoid angering the shades of their ancestors.

We found the same continuity in the motions of the women spinning cotton and the men pounding bark to make clothing. But we also saw elements borrowed from the Spanish invaders, and so felt like witnesses at a cultural breakdown.

It was only after we had lived with the Chacobos for three weeks that the women of the Kako group stopped running away at our approach. Although they couldn't know the result of our operation, they did not often let us photograph them or, when they did grant us this favor, they posed so unwillingly that it was hardly worth insisting. I noticed that they were very agile and quick-footed in taking care of themselves: they didn't need to bend down to collect a bit of vine, a half-eaten ear of corn, or to keep a distaff spinning. They knew how to weave and to fire clay.

I spent the morning recording a myth and about thirty words in the Chacobo dialect (Panoan language). Little by little, I'm adding to my native vocabulary: *Ouche,* the moon. *Wari,* the sun. *Ounoupacha ,* water. *Noora boté,* I am a friend.

All around, nature seems impelled by a terrible thirst: the rivers twist and change shape. Schools of piranhas slash through them searching for prey. Unlike other regions of the Amazon—although it may be no more than a legend?—these carnivorous fish do not cause many accidents. They may be voracious and aggressive, but the Indians are more afraid of candirus, eels, and fluvial rays. (Candirus are minuscule fish that enter the bather's body through the most intimate orifices; this can cause death. The eel is equipped with electric organs that give shocks strong enough to paralyze a limb, and their strike can lead to drowning. The tail of the fluvial ray possesses a venomous barb, which it uses to inflict a deep wound to anyone who disturbs it.)

Perched in a tree, on one of the branches that hangs above the water and the rushes growing alongside, the Indian waits patiently for fish.

He spits in the water to amuse himself. The least ripple launches a sequence of "chain reactions": his head retracts between his shoulders, the muscles of his face contract, his bow moves imperceptibly, and the tip of his arrow points toward the shadows gliding through the rushes. They are *tucunarés.* Before firing, he adjusts his position slightly to compensate for the error due to refraction....

The Chacobo Indians are more than willing to catch fish by stunning them—using a poison extracted from a yellowish root—because it offers the double advantage of being less tiring and often quite a bit more successful. They gather the roots (*Tephrosia toxicaria*) and grind them between two hardwood logs; the product is placed in a gourd where it is diluted. Then it is a matter of pouring it into a pool of stagnant water, waiting twenty minutes, and gathering the poisoned fishes. Since the mixture affects only cold-blooded animals, not man, the fish are still perfectly edible, the poison doesn't even change their flavor.

Fishing, hunting, food gathering. Thus, the whole year round, these "jungle hoboes" live by their wits.... We—we whose existence is a living death—do not know how to experience the tranquil poverty of these Indians: it is another way of being human, another world.

How long have we been here? We have forgotten to keep track of the days, but it must be—as *our* Indians would say—more than "two moons." We have run out of everything. Assaulted by a commonplace evil: hunger. Things look grim, and if the Chacobos had not volunteered their help, the situation would have been critical. Our hosts advise us to build a raft of balsa trunks, to flee this place before the river goes down; they propose to attempt the adventure on another boat. Our supplies are exhausted, so we don't have much choice. We count the miles: one hundred seventy-five to Paredon, thirty to cross the savannah to reach the Madeira River, then another hundred to get to Guayaramerin. Paradoxically, by measuring the distance we have to travel, we feel we are leaving behind this little world without history.

Morale is low. Throughout the evening, I am haunted by some words that seem appropriate, this verse by Paul Lecointe:

> Dieu te bénisse
> Si par malheur
> Instant critique
> Sur un vapeur
> Pour l'Amérique
> Tu pars un jour.

[God help you /if you should happen/one fatal moment/to find yourself/ on a boat to America/someday.]

and this by Lévi-Strauss:

> Amazone, chère Amazone,
> Vous qui n'avez pas de sein droit
> Vous nous en racontez de bien bonnes
> Mais vos chemins sont trop étroits.

[Amazon, dear Amazon/you don't have an honest heart/you tell us of wonderful things/but the way to them is too hard.]

20 June

While I'm forcing myself to write in this journal, in a country where the sun seems to oppose all efforts, even mental ones, I see Nako—an Indian boy of about fourteen—and Jacques C. go into the forest; they are going out in search of the parrot—or agouti, or monkey—which will form the sum of our single daily meal.

That night: hunger has made us cruel and a little crazy. Jacques and Nako have brought back a large rodent, a red *jochi;* we skin it, laughing wildly, and we tear off a leg, the share due to Nako. We are smeared with blood....

In front of the cooking pot where some chunks of agouti, three green bananas, some globs of brown rice are simmering together, we decide to leave this place as quickly as we can. Our hosts are right: we can't even consider going by land. There are three main arguments against it: the materials we've gathered, which we do not want to abandon, the lack of trails connecting us to the so-called civilized world, and the reluctance of the Chacobo to travel any distance from their territory. The only possible solution: to go down the Yata River. On a raft? Why not?

Night falls. Insects become more and more numerous and we are soon forced to take refuge under our mosquito netting. My pipe is irremediably empty.

21 June

We've told Maro, the chief of this group of Chacobos, about our plan and asked his advice. He is skeptical. He thinks we're incompetent. (Long ago, Vaca Diez was not able to convince the Araona to go with him down the Beni River. They refused him in these words: "How can you envisage such a voyage? We who are men, even we would not take such a trip lightly." Surprised, Vaca Diez asked, "Why are you men and we're not?" The Araona replied: "It's a well-known fact that you have only one wife, while the least able among us has at least four!") Our conversation went without too many hitches; over the past weeks we've been able to pick up bits and ends of the Chacobo dialect. Maro himself, through his occasional meetings with hunters pursuing ocelots and caymans, had learned a few words of Spanish. "*Es mucho, mister ... Es mucho,*" he told us. But he did indicate a part of the forest where we could find the trees "to make a raft," some balsam trees.

A frugal meal of the rest of the agouti, then we went into the forest to look for the famous trees. We got turned around, retraced our steps ten times, in a sensual and disturbing labyrinth; the animals took cover at our approach. Two hours of prospecting. Then, there it was! Above us loomed smooth gray trunks, a grove of balsams.

The job of felling and cutting them. Not very used to plying an ax, and despite the softness of the wood, we came back dead tired; ten trees cut down and no fewer blisters on our hands.

22 June

The balsam grove is starting to look like a lumber camp. The cut trees have dragged along some epiphytes as they fell, but the vegetation is so dense that they haven't reached the ground and hang suspended between brambles and orchids. Then we have to cut them to the desired length, eleven and a half feet, and remove the bark, which, torn in strips, will serve as trim for the trunks.

Thursday, 23 June

We've sliced a track through the jungle with our machetes. Many, many mosquitoes and "tucandaras" ants. We feel a terrible fatigue from these last three months of life in the wild. Tonight: green bananas again! Why, after all, aren't bananas allowed to ripen before they are eaten in this country?

Friday, 24 June

Around three o'clock. Backs bruised, shoulders aching, we admire the twenty-one trunks lined up in the sun; we will let them dry for three or four days. We still have to cut the cross-pieces that will stretch across the balsas logs and to choose the vines to tie the raft together.

26 June

We have traded a mirror, some beads, and a big pair of scissors for some manioc; this large tuberous root has a flavor between a chestnut and a potato. The dry season is just starting, the best weather is the end of August and the first few days of September. The muddy waters are still floating with trees and isles of greenery, with *canuelas*. The water level is starting to go down and the lagoon on which the village is built no longer connects to the Yata River except by a channel too narrow for our raft. We have spent the afternoon moving the trunks one at a time so they will fit through the channel. Our last chloroquine capsules (to prevent malaria) have disappeared mysteriously. No mistake, it's these brats who have stolen them from us. But what would they want with them? They know perfectly well how much good is done by the green-and-white pastilles we give them for fever. We make a brief inventory and establish another theft: a tube of toothpaste. Upon investigation, it turns out that Nako, who had gone out as hunting partner with J.C., had filched it from us and then gone off and gulped down the contents!

27 June

Étachi, abandoning his manioc patch, has come to help us put the finishing touches on our raft. (We've already built it and christened it *Silbaco*.) In mud to midthigh, we are tying the trunks together in two places, using vines; the whole thing seems strong enough to survive the hundred miles of river between us and the place where we will be able to continue our course to Guayaramerin on the Mamoré River. The leeches are taking advantage of this to suck a little bit of European blood, the bastards!

28 June

Today we are going to set out on the Yata River. We are drinking chicha one last time; the Chacobo women make chicha by chewing corn meal, which they then spit into an earthenware jar (oh, the nasty cliche!). The Chacobo cross the lagoon to accompany us to the raft moored at the edge of the river. Men, women, and children risk capsizing, and all pile into unstable canoes, hollowed out of mahogany trunks. Midday. Full sun. We entrust our 35-mm camera Kuya for a farewell photo; we will find out when it gets developed if he centers the picture and does not wiggle too much, the way we showed him. The "new hoboes"—as we refer to them among ourselves—make some timid gestures: our launch hesitates before entering the strongest part of the current. The die is cast.

Two hours later. The Yata River twists and meanders, and we are only fifteen minutes away from the Chacobo village on foot. Still there are no signs of the presence of man. The rivers are low, but can flood in the rainy season: this is rubber-tree country. It is also the domain of long-legged pink-and-white wading birds, of river tortoises, of caymans. We know this part of the river well, we have come here to hunt with the Indians many times.

Around five in the afternoon a pair of dolphins appear, good-sized animals, between six and a half and eighty feet. For a long time we are able to watch them swim alongside us about forty feet from our boat. During one long trip on the Mamoré River, we managed to photograph these large freshwater mammals, gentle and friendly.

Our expedition proved to be more unpleasant than we had imagined. The moments were rare when we could savor the peace and quiet, the amazing privilege of living an adventure from another age. At first we had to suffer the plague, the constant assault of the maringouins, insects about the size of gnats, whose bites leave red marks dotting the skin. We looked like we had smallpox. When it was almost dark, they retired, leaving the field to the inevitable mosquitoes. I'm choosing my words carefully when I write (what comfort): mosquitoes are filthy beasts. They torment us like the most terrible toothache! (One day I must write a broadside attacking mosquitoes.)

Malaria: trembling knowledge of Amazonia.

A few moments after the disappearance of the dolphins, as we were going into a long curve, the wind pushed us toward the bank and our raft was caught in a whirlpool.

We didn't have any oars, and there was no way to control our direction; we took turns diving into the river to push the raft back into the current. The results were disappointing; the wind proved more tenacious than us. After a good quarter of an hour at this exhausting game, we gave up, shivering with cold under the pale late afternoon sun.

We spit out a good dozen oaths. The bulge of river by the curve where the wind had blown us opened onto a brackish lagoon, a dead arm that disappeared a few hundred meters into the forest. We watched helplessly as the wind pushed us toward it. Far away, the river seemed as remote as the Dordogne to us.

Awful moment of depression—of frustration. We considered the situation. We were in the middle of nowhere. No one would ever come to our rescue and in two hours it would be dark. We towed the raft using branches and plants that grew in the river. Our progress was slow but steady.

Seven o'clock at night. The sun is going down behind some tall trees. We have nibbled away at more than two miles; at last, our boat points down-river again and the current takes hold of us. Joy on board.

About the finished raft or *callapo* (the Guarani word): it is a launch eleven and a half feet long, more than six and a half feet wide. The entire back section—we call it the "stern" even though neither the wind nor the current respects this distinction—is occupied by a cabin where we are going to spend the night. Inside it we have stored the technical material collected on our expedition; we are being very careful with it. We lay a fire in the front of the platform.

Tonight's menu did not take long to compose: manioc cooked over the hot coals. There's not much.

For the night, we will take turns on watch. I will take the first shift, from seven o'clock until one-thirty in the morning. Jacques C. will take the hours until dawn.

The wind dies down and navigation becomes simpler, more mechanical. J. C. goes to lie down, but after the events of the day, he can't get to sleep. He comes back to the "bridge" and we sit in silence for a long time watching dark shapes and shadows glide by. We take an electric torch and shine it on the banks of the river to spot caymans, whose eyes seem to flare up in the dark, only to be extinguished.

Have you ever watched a bit of match floating in a gutter? That was us. The raft spins, turns on itself, and suddenly runs up against the branches of an uprooted tree, leaning out of the eroded riverbank. The stronger current in these places increases the danger of capsizing. We can't keep from picturing the consequences of a mistake in maneuvering the raft. Without food or weapons, on a deserted river, we would never make it back to the Indians, or to the rubber camp at Paredon, at least a week's walk through the deadly jungle. Our only hope would be don Renato, his boat is the only one that travels along the Upper Yata, above the point where it meets the Benicito. But it's too late in the year for him. The water is too low, exposing "hidden bars," solitary rocks that jut out into the river and form an obstacle to any boat that draws water. In high water, these bars are entirely submerged and their location is marked by fairly easy rapids.

Working feverishly, we hack at the branches with a machete. The raft pushes its way through this breach, creaks, finally frees itself and resumes its halting and twisting course.

29 June

Two o'clock in the morning. After a few hours of sleep, Jacques C. begins his turn on watch. Nothing to report. He dozes on the bridge, keeping the fire going and half-opening an eye from time to time. We go through a rapid without too much damage.

Six-thirty in the morning. I wake up to discover a humid dawn, the day still vibrant with the chatter of huge wading birds. With the sun, the wind also comes up and chases the mist away and blows us back into a lagoon just like the one the night before. Adventure does not spoil us for routine events. We have our technique down and we have overcome our anxiety: all we have to do is resist fatigue, hunger, pain, and we are sure to free our boat.

Four hours of hard work and forced swims; the *Silbaco* is back floating with the current and carrying us once more toward the world of men. Jacques C. makes this reflection: "This boat, the *Silbaco,* is our escape hatch." We shall see.

During the few quiet moments, we bring out a cane fishing pole and start casting in hope of improving our menu. I catch a piranha about eight inches long. Removing the hook is a delicate operation, because the piranha has an extremely strong jaw and sharp pointy little teeth—the Moré Indians of the Itenez River area use them to make scissors. Jacques C., who was bitten once, takes elaborate precautions.

Another piranha bites through the nylon line, and we lose the last hook we had left. We have to add eight inches of metal wire to the end of the line....

Accomplishing a hazardous maneuver, we succeed in beaching the raft. We get off and walk around to collect firewood and cook dinner.

> Menu for 29-6-1966:
> Piranha cooked over live coals (for two)
> Very salty brown rice
> Manioc, Indian-style

This meal followed a lengthy nostalgic discussion centering on the subject of camembert and new Beaujolais.

We had noted the presence of a number of "water trees"; cut into them in the right spot and a jet of water gushes out, rain water stored inside each stalk, at the base of every leaf. These trees are *patuyu,* false banana trees. They are natural reservoirs where one can find water that's potable, if not fresh, in all seasons. We frequently make do with the muddy water from the river and risk amoebic dysentery. It's night again. Guard duty has fallen to J.C. But suddenly there's a storm, a strong wind rises, making us drift toward a new obstacle: a tangle of dead trees and bamboo. This *surazo,* a cold wind from the south, makes us forget that we are at the thirteenth parallel, well above the Tropic of Capricorn.

Navigation becomes impossible. The surface of the river is covered with little waves, quick and sharp. We spend the rest of the night washed up on an island of sand that the receding waters had exposed in the middle of the river.

A few drops start to fall.

30 June

We are awakened by rain. Quickly, we pull oilskin to cover the cabin; the thin roof of palm fronds is leaking water everywhere; a violent storm beats down on us, soaking our covers, our pallets made of leaves. This is one of the last rains before the absolute dryness of the other season, July-August-September. It stays with us all morning.

When it comes time to light the fire, we can't find the matches and tinderbox. Failed acts multiply: a bad sign. Troubling too, because according to our estimates, we are still three days from the ranch at Paredon. We go over our actions carefully, in detail. We locate the tinderbox, good and dry, in a waterproof camera bag....

More and more often, our silent progress allows us to get close to the river's white ducks, the *roncadores.* Our carbine is not equipped with a sight scope, which might have been useless in the forest where the vegetation is too thick and the light too feeble, but would have been very useful here: we fire several cartridges without success.

Around five in the afternoon, we spy a couple of *mutun* turkeys on a tiny beach. I fire at them from close range. I've hit one of them. Self-satisfied look and shouts of joy. Trying to flee, the big black winged creature falls into the water and is swept away on the current. Impossible to get to him quickly, Jacques C. throws off his clothes and plunges in. Just as he reaches the beach, I see him go limp, then collapse. Is it a cramp or ...?

Nothing serious ... he swims back to the callopo in a few strokes, and I help him lift himself onto it. After which, it's my turn to dive in to fish out the turkey, which by this time is long gone, lost from view. It would be too stupid, considering the circumstances, to let our piece of good luck drift away.

Back on board. Jacques C. has already lost a lot of blood; there is a deep gash in his right foot: the spotted ray does not forgive the man who disturbs its rest. What should we do? Our first aid kit was emptied while we were staying with the Chacobo; no more disinfectant, no antibiotics. All we have left are a few bandaids and sticking plasters. We boil some water. (The ranch at Paredon is still three days' travel away....)

The pain persists, unbearable. My companion swears furiously at the turkey, the spotted ray, and the Amazon. Me, I pluck furiously at the turkey.

1 July

Calm night. We slept without worrying about the progress of our raft. Today I was responsible for navigating the raft by myself. Jacques C. feels awful. His foot is terribly swollen and he can't stand up on it. Fortunately, the pain eased six hours after the accident. The wound is not yet infected, but we fear the worst. We don't talk about it. We are traveling toward a herd of cabay, aquatic rodents that can reach a length of a meter and a third. Along the Beni, the meat of the cabay or capibara is not esteemed very highly. Our personal opinion is that fresh game is only too rare: we get out our .22 long rifle. Some shots ring out. One cabay, bleeding from the head, in its death throes, spins round and round on the surface of the water, but we cannot catch it. Just as we decide that it has gotten away from us, the animal's strength gives out and it lets itself be carried away by the current, which pulls it into our path. We drag it on board. It must weigh at least twenty-five pounds, several day's food. We have exactly twenty-seven bullets left for our .22.

Night of the 1ˢᵗ to 2ᵈ

We have completely eliminated night watches. We both sleep, awakened again and again by shuddering stops, snapping branches, and strange sounds. A tree crashes down two inches from our raft. In the darkest part of the night, we get caught in a whirlpool several hundred yards across, a nauseating merry-go-round; we watch the raft turn round on itself. This time, is there any way out? The shore is far off, hostile; the night deep blue and green. Discouraged by this new piece of bad fortune, we go back into our cabin, to put off confronting the problem until tomorrow. About three hours later, water floods into the cabin; we rush out. There we were, tangled in the branches of an *ochoo* tree. We free the *Silbaco* without too much difficulty. We had the good fortune to escape the whirlpool … in our sleep.

2 July

When we get up, we find, floating near us, the cadaver of a tapir with swollen belly and rigid legs. The animal was probably wounded by hunters and drowned while trying to escape them. It couldn't have been dead more than two days. We had enough salt to dry the meat in the sun, as they do in eastern Bolivia (to make jerky): I dive in and haul the tapir back to carve it up. Only poetry makes us renounce this necrophagous food. Eyes darkened; cheeks hollow: we are completely outside civilization.

3 July

Saw a couple of marabous with red throats—the way they pose in the water is both regal and ridiculous—and farther off, a noisy troupe of monkeys. The Yata is a huge game preserve. The forest is becoming thinner: it is no more than a delicate screen of trees along the river's edge. The next area we travel through is pampa, where there are only tall grasses and stunted trees, where pumas roam, and herds of wild boars, *taitetu,* and ostriches. Now and again, in these vast deserted stretches, we see a cattle ranch. We think we hear, faintly, the barking of a dog, and then later the lowing of cattle. The ranch at Paredon cannot be very far. But we don't see anything. The curtain of trees adds a few looping meanders. At the end of our sixth night on the river: from the far end of the cabin where I am lying, I can see the bearded face of Jacques C., lit by the fire where he is cooking a cabay joint. All of a sudden, the roof of a house detaches itself from a sky speckled with stars and fireflies. Paredon. About time! One last anxious moment. Will the current keep us from landing? On the high bank where we manage to pull ashore, a shadowy woman watches us. It's not very much, it's enough.

Eight days later we reach Guayaramerin, and Jacques Chabert, whose wound is threatened by gangrene, undergoes emergency surgery in a clinic run by Doctor Bravo. During his four weeks of convalescence, I'm going to take a trip up the Guaporé River, where I've been told there are "savages," the Moré Indians. A lie: they wear white shirts and pants. Ready to shed their clothes for a bottle of liquor.…

I travel around South America, taking a zigzag route: Uruguay, Chile,

Brazil, Argentina. With a companion, Robert Bexiga, I visit the Guayaki Indians of Paraguay. Then always searching for Indians who are truly primitive, I head for the Peruvian Amazon.

The Purus River, all twists and turns, moves blindly through a cloak of vegetation that is always green—and more out of date with each season—in that infamous Eden of explorers and pioneers, the jungle. They strode in wearing heavy Dutch velvets and starched collars, with but one goal, to obtain gold and spices, but all they actually found were small troublesome beasts, fevers, and, to complete the trick, unyielding bands of Indians, ephemeral love, at best a little rubber to help pay for the deception. "It's cold as a vault!" wrote one Frenchman. At dusk, at the hour when beauty fades, we strike up against a rampart of sand, and there, stranded, run aground on that point, we fall asleep, not even troubling to remove our shoes. In the image of the forest, our bodies. They blend with the trees, the animals, the elements. The damp shade has penetrated them. That is all.

In Amazonia, sadness spreads through the trees. Its forests, where the most ordinary exoticism is like a painting; its waters, mirrors of our poor dreams, capture the eyes of the adventurer.

Little by little, the absinthe of the tropics goes to one's head.... Then no lyricism is equal to this dream garden; tangle of vines and tree ferns, eruption of palms caught in the bulge of the earth. Does one dare, with these few words, these feeble adjectives, try to sketch such a landscape?

The dark line of a thunderstorm cuts across the sky; in October, clear spells are brief, high humidity is permanent. We are traveling up the Curanja, a tributary of the Upper Purus, and the hours vanish in sweeping strokes of the oars. We watch for a garden patch in a burnt clearing, a moored dugout, a banana plantation or a palm roof, the first unmistakable sign of the presence of the people who own this place: the Cashinahua Indians.

AYAHUASCA: LSD OF THE JUNGLE

"First, you will feel chills, you'll have pain in your temples and in the center of your forehead. And then, you will see some lovely things, you will see the dead, many people.... As for me, what frightens me is serpents.

Kana-Maroeti leans his head toward the torch in the center of the hut;

sometimes he bites his lower lip, stops speaking, and stares at me without blinking.

"A little *cawa* will plunge you into darkness, you have to add *nichi-paeu* to see the boas and the houses with huge windows."

Nichi-paeu: the name refers to a vine whose branching stem climbs to the roof of the forest. In the camps in the Upper Yata, among the Chacobo, the women use it to treat conjunctivitis and eczema of the eyelid, others brew it in a potion for the treatment of certain types of ulcers. I point it out to my informant—but, in fact, does he understand my pidgin blend of Spanish and Cashinahua? Kana-Maroeti continues:

"Yes, it's a vine. Cawa is a leaf. I know how to prepare nichi-paeu cawa."

We catch on. He's talking about a drug, common in the western Amazon, which the Indians use for hallucinogenic purposes: *ayahuasca.* In Quechua, purportedly the language of the Incas, the word means "vine of the dead" or "vine of the spirits"; however—at the risk of depoeticizing this sweet flower of alchemy and savage thought—the name could also be no more than a corruption of *ayak-huasca,* "bitter vine." Other names are commonly used for this same type of drug: *caapi, yagé (yaxé* or *yajé),* and in Brazil, *timbo branco.*

Because the experience of the drug can get lost in interpreting, or commenting on it, we will provide some information about ayahuasca. In the eighteenth century, R. P. José Chantre Herrera was the first to describe its usage: "The diviner puts his bed in the middle of the house or erects a platform and places alongside it a diabolical brew the Indians call ayahuasca, which has a singular power to make a man lose consciousness." One must wait until the next century for a description of the plant, by Richard Spruce, an English botanist, based on the plant collections sent to Europe. Recently, since drugs are the order of the day, scientists have been trying to identify the active principle, the *flower power,* and then made this substance the subject of numerous chemical, pharmacological, and clinical experiments. Without waiting for the experts to reach their conclusions, tribal communities of hippies—calling it yagé—have made it a remedy for their mal de demi-siècle.

It took us a morning to find the two plants; Konpri, the civil chief of the Balta community, turned up his nose at the cawa plants we found. We had to search for a mature plant. He was less punctilious about the nichi-paeu, only insisting we cut the vine as high as possible and take a cutting to transplant. We returned to the village with three yard lengths of vine and four handfuls of leaves. That afternoon was devoted to the preparation of the drug. Kana-Maroeti started by throwing a handful of cawa leaves into four liters of water; then he cut the vine into fifteen pieces, crushed them between two round logs, and placed them in the cauldron. Three handfuls of cawa leaves were ground fine, then added to the whole leaves and the chunks of vine. A woman kept a blaze going under it. The whole concoction was boiled for forty minutes; then Kana-Maroeti poured the still-steaming liquid through a basket that had a filter of plant fibers arranged in the bottom.

"Nichi-paeu cawa should be drunk cold," he said.

That night I went to the hut of Kana-Maroeti and found several people already there: Énaro, Érakuano, Polichio, Konpri, Kanisa, and Kuka. Konpri said to me:

"You are going to drink nichi-paeu cawa, and soon you will see serpents; when they disappear, you can go back to your hammock.

> Viens doucement, nichi-paeu cawa
> Rends-nous heureux,
> Après va-t'en, va-t'en, va-t'en.

[Come softly, nichi-paeu cawa/make us happy/then go away, go away, go away.]

It was eight-seventeen. I had taken the drug reluctantly, with a false show of bravado, and the stoned look in the eyes of the others disturbed me.... I kept checking my tape recorder, and my watch, and my pulse, and my heart. Nothing. I attributed my anxiety to my favorite prejudice: I hate organized trips. Eight twenty-five.

"It won't take effect for a long time," whispered my neighbor. "While you're waiting, do you want to smoke a pipe?"

Eight-thirty. Polichio begins speaking in a falsetto voice. He stammers out an incomprehensible litany, falling apart; a chant that's not done and not to be done. We lose our sense of time.

Eight thirty-seven. Discussion about which of us is going to tell a story. Kuka prevails. He is going to tell me the legend "The Man in the Lagoon."

The Man in the Lagoon
(as told by Kuka)

A long, long time ago, it happened that a hunter went into the forest, to kill the multicolored birds whose feathers are used to make ceremonial headdresses. He built a blind out of palms on the edge of a lagoon. A toucan came and stood within range of his bow. But, just as the hunter released his arrow, he noticed another animal: a tapir. It was too far away. He contented himself with watching it, hidden behind some branches. The tapir picked three fruit, scooped out the meat, and threw the rest in the lagoon. A boa-woman came out of the water. Dripping wet, huge, and beautiful. The tapir moved immediately to violate her.

"I wish that I could do the same," exclaimed the hunter.

He returned to the village, dreaming about what he had seen, and about the body of the boa-woman....

The next day, the hunter returned to the same place. He picked three fruit, ate the meat, and threw the rest in the lagoon. The woman appeared once more, beautiful creature! He pressed himself upon her, but before he was able to satisfy his need, he felt her transform herself into a boa. She knotted herself around him.

"Don't be afraid, I am really a woman.... I do not have a husband. And you, are you free?"

"Oh ... I am free," he replied.

"Then let's go and live together!"

"But ... I can't."

"Don't be a fool. Just wait and you will see!"

Then she covered his body with little green feathers.

"Hold on to my hair," she told him.

She dove straight for the bottom of the lagoon ... and soon they found themselves in a camp with people and huts and dugout canoes and hammocks and cookpots on the fire.... What clever devils those serpents!

"Mama, I've brought back a man!"

"He could live with us," said the old woman.

The hunter and the boa-woman held their marriage celebration the next day, and the nichi-paeu cawa was prepared.

"Do not drink any of that," said the young bride, "it is sure to make you scream." The hunter protested, said that he was a brave man, and insisted that his parents-in-law fill a gourd for him. After he drank, he was assaulted by bright images, numerous caymans, and a swarm of snakes. "Oh ... oh ... oh ...," he cried at the top of his lungs. Then, like the day after a festival, all became quiet.

"I have seen some boas!"

"That was us," said the boa-woman.

Many moons went by, and the man learned to live with the boas. As a boa.

The first wife of the hunter came to weep at the edge of the lagoon. A tiny fish overheard her sad story. After some time this fish chanced to meet the hunter and so was able to tell him of the suffering of his abandoned wife.

"Your children are dying of hunger," said the fish. "Men weren't meant to live under the water. Come back to land, right now!"

"But ... I can't."

"Don't be a fool. Just wait and you will see!"

Then the fish covered his body with little green feathers.

"Hold on to my hair," the fish told him.

The little fish jumped straight out of the lagoon, and soon they found themselves in a camp with people and huts and dugout canoes and hammocks and cookpots on the fire.... Among men!

"Papa has come back," cried a little girl's voice.

"Where were you?" asked his wife.

"Oh ... I was kidnapped by the boas."

Two days later, the hunter wanted to go into the woods to look for some wax or some resin to stick the feathers onto his arrows.

"Don't go ... I'm afraid ...," begged his wife.

To no avail. He went off and his journey led him to the edge of the lagoon. There, a baby boa rushed up to meet him....

"Oh, Papa! Why did you go away? Come back home!"

The baby boa caught hold of his foot but wasn't able to pull him in. An adult boa came to help, but the hunter had had a chance to grab on to a vine and nothing could make him let go of it. The serpent swallowed him, up to his waist. Off in the opposite direction, the men of his village heard his cries, and followed them to the accursed lagoon. They killed the huge boa and freed the man from his dreadful position.

Unfortunately, the hunter remained paralyzed.

"Go look for some nichi-paeu and some cawa," he told the other men.

The men came back with all sorts of vines, all sorts of leaves, because they did not know anything about these two plants. So then, before he died, the hunter taught them the secrets of nichi-paeu cawa.

("The Man in the Lagoon," in its complete version, plays a central role in Cashinahua mythology and has a number of ramifications for their society. The legend describes the origin of poetry, explains the decorative motifs in tribal art, and is probably linked to rules about hunting. In fact, among the Huni-kui, boas are protected; there is a prohibition against killing them.)

Nine-o-five. I had felt the first symptoms long before Kuka had finished his story. First, stomach cramps. Shivering. And then, while my internal organs seemed to twist themselves into knots, some shooting pains along my spine and bursts of light before my eyes. Confused senses. Vomiting. Things took on a marvelous complexity. Two or three times, by myself, I tried to understand. A rush, a glissade of thoughts. A solo voice—Polichio? —struggled to cross the few meters separating us; it reached me as a chorus of buzzing. I decided to take some notes. My watch spins out an unusual beat: four seconds by four seconds. I dance without stopping. I am happy. I hear the roar of a swarm of colors. They flash when I close my eyes, and shimmer. Boas? No, blue ants. I do not know anymore. My five senses are not enough. Everything is blue. I have reached the outer limits of myself.... View from an airplane: bodies of water entwine under a blue counterpane, thick and leafy, and the trees open only for the space of a clearing between two storms. My visions keep dissolving: the drug has me under its spell, I know it, it enchants me. And *I see myself* sailing over some spilled ink, *I see myself* wandering among a flurry of flowers. I want to call out to myself: sleepwalker, the nights are blue! What is this vibrating between us? ... (For more than an hour, I was in a state of euphoria, during which time it was impossible for me to write or even express the slightest thought.)

Nichi-paeu cawa goes away. It makes me think of a common image: a young girl putting out a fire with a handful of snow.

I go back to my hammock. It's over: the session had lasted three hours.

At first, one takes drugs with an aesthetic purpose. The poverty of the initial experience must be attributed to the naïveté of the project, the lack of knowledge, the unusual nature of the challenge, that is, to the psychological ground—waste or fallow—on which the drug falls. "Thus, the man trolling for treasure pulls up herrings instead of gold nuggets," laments Du Bellay. Closer to our time, Henri Michaux voices his complaint at the very beginning of a very beautiful book: "Drugs bore us with their paradise. Better they should give us a little knowledge. This is not the golden age." No, it's the age of experimentation.

Ayahuasca, the most common, is not the only hallucinogenic drug in the Amazon basin. Several other names spring to mind: *toe-ihuanga, hucho-sanango, chiri-sanango,* and *ayac-sanango.* Primarily of plant origin, all these drugs contain alkaloids—the same substance as nicotine, caffeine, cocaine, quinine—and all are being tested to identify their components. There has already been a lot of ink spent on articles describing ayahuasca from this point of view: three names—télépathine, yaguéine, and banistérine—have been assigned to the alkaloids isolated from the plants studied by the first researchers. These scientists go further, to state that the principal active ingredient can be reduced to a single harmine. The most recent experiments do prove that harmine plays an important role, but that does not mean that the presence of other substances should be ignored.... Finally, turning to a subject that interests us, it is necessary to explain the use of the drug among primitive peoples and to measure its cultural incidence. Nothing could be more difficult, because the drug is a magic bag that can expand to hold anything; it's bottomless, an abyss. Where we encountered it, along the Purus River, it is used as a stimulant, providing extra strength during initiation ceremonies. It is reputed to restore the virility of old men. It helps the Indians discover the tricks of fate; it tells them how and when to launch an attack on their enemies. It lets them catch a glimpse of "houses with huge windows," and of caymans and boas and jaguars and trees heavy with fruit. It brings the dead back to life, as well. That is why it is frequently offered during funeral ceremonies.... One point, on its medicinal use: ayahuasca is not a cure in itself. The shaman prescribes it as an aid, but language is still the best medicine he provides. In its most modern usage, the drug has become a means of escape, of compensation. It is the refuge of poorly assimilated groups that have lost their traditional ways.

Soon, the law and the missionaries will prevail, and ayahuasca will be viewed as nothing more than a narcotic....

FROM AYAHUASCA TO ASHES: I surprised him in front of his hut made of branches. Lost in a dream, in thoughts that aren't thought, in the ancient wisdom of the myths; the savage smokes his pipe, taking tiny puffs. In all simplicity, in silence, like the sand running through an hourglass.... His face has the mark of a healer, a diviner of fate, and he gives me a look that would like to be evil. Then, since it's the custom, he invites me to smoke with him. We pass the short pipe back and forth a few times, we talk, and, finally, we even laugh. (Haven't we consumed a "small burnt offering"?)

Tobacco, like the drug, performs wise miracles.

I stayed several months in the Peruvian valley of Upper Purus, at the point south of the Loreto, among the different tribes that lived there: the Culina, the Sharanahua, the Marinahua, the Mastenahua, the Cashinahua, and the Amahuaca.

The Mastenahua, who live along the right bank of the river, share the worst fate of all the indigenous forest dwellers of the Amazon: hunger, poverty, and hatred. Their tribe has been reduced to a dozen families, to which group has been added a few individuals from other tribes (five Sharinahua, three Marinahua, two Pachonahua, and a Cashinahua woman). Their culture has not suffered from this diversity. Mastenahua, the dialect, is part of the huge Pano family of Indian languages spoken in territories straddling the borders of Bolivia, Brazil, and Peru.

Hunters and small farmers, they survive on the margins of a world that is constantly both soliciting and, in the case of itinerant traders, exploiting them. They are now exposed to the demands of mercantile colonization, to concessions, and, finally, to a painful submission: the objects that they obtain in exchange for beautiful skins—jaguar, ocelot, peccary—display the stamp of a certain ironmongery ethic. Today, exoticism is impure.

The Mastenahua have passed through three linguistic revolutions, indifferent to the appeals and promises of the *nahua* (outsiders): first came the Jesuit priests, then the Peruvian rubber merchants, and nowadays, it's traders with—the latest thing—transistor radios! These tests, five centuries of colonization, have not diminished the vibrant tone of their folklore.

Clearly, death—biological or cultural—is lying in wait for them. So much civilization, terror, contamination, and disease have reached deep in their forests, unsettling them, that they have lost the desire to live. The evil can no longer be controlled. Only tradition, a pitiful flickering flame, saves them from banality and a final decline. There is still time....

I look back at my notes on their face painting, but—in all truth—these gaudy faces, covered with graffiti, with colors, with signs, with shapes, do not yield their full meaning. This painting should not be confused with makeup, or with antique masks. It is not a matter of repair or restoration or reconstruction of a "lost paradise," or of a false face. No, instead, the charm of some, the mystery of others, the red and the black indicate the wish to complete their features—enhancing them, joining them, and making them into a celebration. "I paint myself. My wife paints herself. It is beautiful!" said Uskao simply. To paint, to be painted, is a social act. The tribe, which sets itself up as guardian of myths, requires the artist to follow traditional patterns; only a scrupulous imitation of these themes can guarantee the accomplishment, the efficacy of the work. Faces painted or emblazoned. Singular forms of identity and paradox, the Mastenahua disguise themselves the better to be recognized.

Of course, a more careful study of the themes, a close analysis of a specific pattern, as it relates to age, sex, or tribal status, could reveal the foundations of humanity: the horror of the natural state. I am convinced that, above all else, the facial paintings of the Mastenahua are strongly differentiated along sexual lines and that once the material is elaborated, the significant constants in it will be obvious. The man identifies himself with his role as hunter and quite often places himself under the sign of the jaguar. As for the women, they respond to the call of the man—of the jaguar—by making themselves into prey or bait. The two sexes carry on a conversation this way—face to face—they maintain a dialogue whose refinements no longer come as a shock to me. The savage is not what his name implies.

Kafoe: a composition without corrections. The field of her face is divided into three sections. Asymmetrically, with the nose as axis. The choice of symbols springs from a rebus or a pun: a caterpillar on the right, a butterfly on the left. To achieve distinctness and diversity in the forms she uses to express herself, the woman has taken her inspiration from the stages of metamorphosis. Caterpillar (chrysalis)—butterfly. She has made it an accessory to her beauty, and then has no choice but to go further, and share her joy in exhibiting it. Uskao, her husband, isn't fooled. "Her *keudia* (decoration) pleases me," he confesses laughing.

Rau: a stylized jaguar. The hunter is chasing after a waking dream, luck: what allows him to find game, to shoot well, to be virtually infallible. Never has he accepted returning empty-handed. That is why, in the image of his model the jaguar, he has underlined his eyes in black. Here are the qualities he invokes: flexibility, lightning speed, coolheadedness, cruelty. Certainly, Rau is more than a hunter, but wearing this mask, he is only a hunter.

The men shave carefully, cut their hair back, in order—they told me— to have more surface to paint. They spend long hours hammering a thin piece of metal between two stones to produce the nasal disk (*rucho*) they insert, concocting with great patience feather headdresses they will never wear, and trying to recreate, with their tongues between their teeth, the intricate patterns of a boa or an ocellus or a butterfly's wing. Play provides their center of gravity.

The media used in their art, rudimentary and few in number, depend on the geographic region where they live. A berry as big as a tangerine gives them their black paint—*huito*. *Urucu*—with which they paint themselves red—is provided by the seeds from a cultivated plant; they use it without preparation or mixed with beeswax. And, in addition, the Mastenahua routinely stain their teeth black; for this, they chew the leaves of the *yanamuco*.

I know an old saw: primitives live by the sign of the moon. Westerns, cartoons, Sunday supplements, my concierges, lastly, all the best-informed people swear by it. The moon, it is god of the hordes. I was the last person to question it. So, when I was living with the Mastenahua, I waited for the full moon with the calm authority of my irony. It came in mid-November.

17 November

I get up early, warm a chunk of parrot meat over the coals. It is quite tough. I wash it down with strong, unsweetened lemon juice. Glance at the water: the Purus River, still muddy, rose about fifteen centimeters overnight; a cortege of dead trees, gloomy floats, drift past. Clouds, a slight breeze.

I am not much good at stringing a story together. I try for the fifth time to transcribe a Cashinahua myth, "The Man in the Lagoon." Whole sections of it elude me. I would have to translate it into slang, or add an accent, or do a pastiche of Giono, for any of its sense to reach the ears of outsiders (the nahua). I let myself be distracted by some scolding birds. Finally, to retaliate, I write a nonsense rhyme that kids could sing, or actors in avant-garde shows.

> Adam mordit la pomme
> Trente-deux fois
> A pleines dents
> A pleines dents

Trente-deux fois
Il croqua dedans
Adam n'a qu'une dent.

[Adam bit into the apple/thirty-two times/with all his teeth/all of his teeth/thirty-two times/he fell to it/Adam losing his bite.]

My foolishness cheered me up. I leapt out of my hammock, took down my gun, and headed off to the forest. I ran into Awanako at the place where the first path came out. He asked me for some "good seeds," some tablets, for his son who was having a bad attack of malaria, then he pointed out a spot where he had seen a band of red monkeys. I killed two of them.

When I got back, the camp was in an uproar. Someone had pulled out some feathers. The women were pressing around Tinwarua, who was assigning them jobs; one should run to the fields, another should go pick some berries, one group is eating manioc mush, chewing in unison, and two old ladies are keeping an eye on some peccary joints that are crackling as they roast. All of them, even the dogs, are jumping and leaping about. "We are expecting the Marinahuas," a little girl shouts to me.

In fact, they do arrive. Curiously got up in their Sunday best, half-dressed, with watery eyes and rowdy voices. A bit drunk. I greet them in Spanish. One of them, Pablo, who has a gold tooth in front, answers me, making a grand speech with extravagant courtesy. Lord, what protocol!

We are invited to share a drink. *Massato* (manioc beer), chicha, *chapo* (an unfermented drink of groundnut and banana). Silence. These encounters between Indians have an indefinable weight, a logic. The smallest gesture becomes a ritual. They are fraught with rules, with laws, and so are almost always celebrations without joy. Their kinship with ancient theater should be emphasized: *man acts there.* And, although I cherish the fellowship of the savages, their relations are so serious that it makes me feel sulky and ill.

Pablo makes a sign to me. He is reproaching me for not making good use of him:

"All the visitors know Pablo. I'm the one who teaches them all about my tribe, the animals, plants.... The gringos [North American linguists] invited me to live with them at Yarina Cocha, they offered to give a sewing machine to my wife, and *I told them everything that they wanted to know.*"

Pablo understood. Pablo, duly converted, has the difficult job of being an Indian....

At three in the morning, we all went back to our digs and the dogs went to sleep in the ashes of the fires we'd just put out. The moon is full.

18 November

Bluish dawn. I am very much afraid that a wind from the south, a *surazo*— a cold wind that can lower the temperature by ten degrees in less than fifteen minutes—is slowly rising and I should get out my flu medicine.

I hear sharp cries from the women, who are chattering among themselves. Then they start singing. One voice dominates—Pouta's—high and tight, while the chorus holds a long sorrowful note behind her. Her voice repeats: "We're going to cut the sugarcane. Wait for us, men. We'll be coming back." We wait.

The men are gathered in the central area of the neighboring village, which belongs to the Marinahua: built on an alluvial mound, some twenty huts overlook the beautiful confluence of the Curanja and the Purus rivers. Palm trees wave against a sky that is beyond description. The Indians, in European dress or cloaked in their basic nudity, are talking in small groups; I get the impression that I've been invited to the church meeting of a very special parish. Hunting stories are being told. We wait.

An old man tugs at my sleeve and pulls me aside, away from the meeting. He wants to exchange an oddly colored parakeet for some tobacco or a little lard. Pablo, always on the lookout for a deal, comes over to stick his nose into the business and contrive to complicate matters. The talk goes on and on; to cut it short, I ask to see the unusual bird. It's a masterpiece of bad taste ... an ornithological scandal. Pablo explains to me:

"You see her. At first, she was green like all the others. Samuela transformed her. He fed her for a long time with a bad poison.... The Peruvians call it *peje torre*. And pffft ... she changed color."

The women come back. Very quickly, the men take their places; they repair their toilettes a bit, mill around, and arrange themselves in three rows. The women appear with baskets heaped with pieces of sugarcane, carry them to an open space, and set them down, there at the feet of the men. They sing. One of them grabs hold of a *kana*—a sugarcane baton—and makes a playful attack on a man, giving him a tap on the shoulder. A chase follows. But just as she's about to be caught, she relays the stick to the others, who shout themselves hoarse and try hard to keep it from him. The man plays against all the women. When he has managed to seize the kana from them, he has to go stand at the edge of the camp, and another man is chosen.

Once the men have all the batons, the roles are reversed. One against all. They don't lose interest until the last kana.... Afterward, boys and girls, it would be best to quote Apollinaire, who—in another latitude—wrote: "C'est la fête.... D'amour on revient paf." ["It's a party.... You run smack into love."]

The Mastenahua hunters return to their home, the women and children follow. From their long faces, and the comments they exchange in low voices, I conclude that they are disappointed, the entertainment was too refined: all in all, they didn't get their fill of revelry. Our semicivilized cousins no longer know how to amuse themselves.

In every hut, I discover the same dissatisfied mood, the same expression on the faces of the men stretched out in their hammocks, a vacant look, worn out.... In fact, they're preparing for another celebration. A real one.

Two monkeys, some shoulders of peccary, some slaughtered tortoise, and some manioc have been placed together on a mat of fresh palm leaves. The hunters exchange animal calls. When they come forward, I see them against the light, and, in all honesty, I have never seen a spectacle more moving. Totally transfigured! There they stand, without plumes or headdresses, in their first European clothing, costumes assembled from patched fragments and finished off with touches of devilry—shoes made of black plastic!—obtained at a stiff price from the adventurers who passed through here. They take two steps forward into the sunlight, hesitate, then, silently, they turn toward us: happy, but abashed as dogs that have been whipped.

The end of the meal is distinguished by a speech by the cacique. It boils down to this: "Let's finish everything off, drink to the very last drop, smoke all the tobacco from Dumi-kuru and Awabanoe (nicknames given to Robert Bexiga and the author of these lines). Let's enjoy the luxury of throwing everything away!" And he concludes: "What an excellent speaker I am!"

His words had carried. An uproar broke out on the women's side, and there was a volley of rotten fruit, dirt, and sticky fibers that surprised the areopagus in their borrowed clothes. First, the men resisted and replied with improvised arguments: overripe bananas, vegetable glop, corn beer, manioc scraps. The furies didn't let them finish their statement. They fired away with everything slimy, sloppy, and slippery, as the brawl assumed an epic quality. Farce on a spectacular scale. Then began a counterattack. Not all the blows were regulation; in the heat of the battle, in hand-to-hand fighting, there was no hiding it, the violence became erotic. The intention was clear: they would fight so they'd have to make up. This reconciliation took place in a mudhole; set in a clearing, in front of the huts, lit by full sun, it became the stage for an act that was—or at least seemed to be—anarchic and spontaneous: a taste for dramatization is not the least seductive aspect of this thought we understand so little, neither its inspirations nor its compulsions. The Mastenahua Indians still know how to make the leap from game to ritual. And so the men splash about, disgusting, enraptured and foamy, and the mud squirts between their toes, and with fumbling hands they disguise the women in statues of silt. The dark aspect of the panoply of the West. No one escapes. It is the feast of good times rediscovered.... The day closes with a communal bath. All this could be described as a denial of exoticism, ours and theirs. This festival was a public display—of their opposition to us and civilization, to the Marinahua, to their own weakness and to novelty. It was a defense, an exorcism, conjuring up the evil that is among them.... What name can I possibly give it without betraying its profound significance? All this could be described as some Indian saturnalia: Mastenahua means "the people who are bound," the slaves. But is it enough to seize on a simple analogy? All this could be described as an agrarian rite: the cult of the Earth Mother and of fertility. Yes, but then.... Night has fallen. And I hear the dogs baying at the full moon....

And the popular imagination? Back home, in Europe, it's all silliness and mindless ditties. In Amazonia, it is much more: the dream of the merchant of sand, utterances without history, tough carnivorous words, collective tinkering, disordered logic, the gadget that never goes out of style, the machine to consume time, the impersonal anecdote, the granary of language (not the language mill), the cluster of images, the fable rolled in the throats of old men.... It obeys the laws of all language and, thinking itself in man, is never lost. Behold, it is myth.

All you have to do is touch a myth with your finger for it to shrink into itself, losing its power of speech and its poetic character. In truth, the challenge would be to collect the myths, and carry them off to a museum, and then forget them there. For myths can't be forgotten.

When a primitive enters the closed circuit of myth, laughing and exclaiming, carried along by the charms of the story, he is in a secret place, listening *directly* to himself. And, as in a dream, he is, simultaneously, the transmitter and the receiver.

All the Mastenahua myths are equally beautiful, set off with inchoate logic; they vie to tell the origin of man, of beasts, of things. They form a complex of histories outside of History, and all of them are linked together by a delicate web of connections. Their teaching function is obvious: they claim to tell why things are the way they are. Moreover, they warn men away from grave error, keeping them from the mistakes that lead to ruin; they are respected by young and old alike.

Myth, foolish to talk about it, isn't it? Here's one, perfectly raw. Listen.

The Myth of the Severed Head
(As told by Naikuroj)

First, I must advise you: it was warm and the girl was sleeping half-naked in a hammock hung from the main beam of the hut. Her brother came in; he was returning from a meeting where he had drunk some manioc beer and smoked some tobacco, and he was a little bit tipsy.

He quickly sniffed out his sister's presence. Under cover of the darkness, he went to her and seduced her. They made love without her recognizing him. He played the same trick on the following nights, and the girl was not entirely displeased. But all the same, she was burning with desire to know the name of her suitor. She thought to herself: "Next time I will put my mark on him...."

Soon, her lover came to her. She pretended to be asleep—she snored , she mumbled in her sleep—and when he pressed himself upon her, she raked her nails across his face several times. The man fled.... (Laughter.)

The next day, the men were preparing for war. They were going to attack a rival group who had kidnapped a child. The men discussed tactics and then filed out, one at a time. The woman watched and waited. The last was a man whose face was covered with black marks. She recognized her brother. She screamed at him: "You will die. Your head will be cut off. Yes, cut clean off!"

The warriors traveled for six long days. On the seventh day, they met the enemy and the brother was killed. His head was mounted on a stake. Seeing it, the warriors decided to abandon the conflict and to return home to protect their women. Only the brother of the man who had had his head cut off remained behind to recover the trophy.

So that night he went out to search for the head. On his way he met a flock of *kukuchi* (fireflies). He captured first one, then two, then three of them. He captured very many of them. His body was covered with them and he glowed in the dark. His enemies, who were lurking in ambush at the start of the trail, saw him and were frightened away. Then the man calmly took possession of the head.

Long before dawn, he was awakened by the head, which was making strange noises.... Ra ... Ra ... Ra.... (Laughter.) The head began to talk:

"Brother, bring me some water! I'm thirsty."

He went several times to get the head a drink.

In the morning, he was seized by panic; he ran away as fast as his legs would carry him, not even knowing where he was going. He entered a strange valley, long and wide, thick with vines and palm trees. Growing there were thirty-six thousand kinds of fruit.... He climbed up one of the trees and picked some of them. Suddenly, the head appeared again:

"Brother, why did you leave me? I'm hungry!"

He gave the head three bunches of fruit, and ran off faster than ever.

"There's a spirit following me. Shut the doors!"

The head arrived soon after.

"Brother, why have you abandoned me? Open the door!"

The whole family was in tears.

"Mama, I want to drink some chapo, I'm thirsty!"

The old woman passed him a gourd through a crack in the wall.

"I'm thirsty!"

They passed him the gourd again. Then the head shook sadly.

"They don't want me anymore. I will transform myself, but into what? I want to turn into a tree.... No, not a tree, the people would come and cut me down. Mama, what am I going to do? I want to become a hole.... No, not a hole, the people would come and make a fire in me. They would burn me. Mama. I want to turn into a yarina plant.... But no, the people would come and harvest my fruit. They would pick me. Mama, give me some black thread."

The woman passed him a full spindle. The head cast the thread into the sky, but it didn't reach very high.

"More black thread! More black thread!" cried the head.

They gave it to him.

"Mama, I'm going to become the moon!"

Before the head had taken its place among the stars, women knew nothing of menstrual blood and pain.

"I will contaminate them, you will see!" proclaimed the head.

When the head had taken its place on high, the men opened their doors and went out. The moon was lighting up the sky. But all the women were soon sick....

In presenting three images of Mastenahua life, no more than partial images, simply juxtaposed, I am not attempting to prove some point. Assembling the elements of my story in this way—the right to beauty, the topsy-turvy ceremony, the myth of the severed head—I do not mean to extract some abstract concept from my empirical knowledge, merely to suggest the flavor of these people's lives. Which is not so easy to do.

Another Story of a Severed Head
(as told by the Piro Indians)

Two Piro Indians were traveling up the Tambo River. They had brought along a basket of provisions: bananas, fish, and dried meat.

To get to the first village upstream, they had to fight against the current with paddle and pole for two long days. They had to endure heat and mosquitoes.

The elder of the two had a bad habit, he always wanted to wait till later to eat, saying: "We must save our food. You never know what might happen."

The first day was very hard and the young Piro was famished.

"I beg of you ... give me something to eat."

"Wait a little while...."

"I'm hungry! I'm hungry!" repeated the boy.

But the old man would not be moved. He decided to go to sleep: he would be strong in the face of misfortune. Early the next morning, he got up and went to bathe. He folded his hammock and his mosquito net. Then he noticed that the young Piro had not yet risen. He lifted the mosquito net to reproach him for his laziness.... Before he had time to say a word, the head of the boy made a great bound and landed on the old man's shoulder, next to his own. No matter how hard he tried, he couldn't manage to get rid of it.

"Now you must take care of me," said the head.

The man arrived at the village with one head too many. He was careful to give it plenty of food, but it absolutely refused to detach itself. At night, when it was time to sleep, the head stood guard next to the mosquito net. Impossible to escape it. A week went by without the head's allowing him a moment's rest. It was hopeless. After a time, the old man went out on a hunt.

"Look at that turkey! Wait for me right here, I'm going to shoot it with my arrow...."

The head agreed to let him go. Free at last, the old man ran away, to a place where the head would not be able to find him. The head called for him in vain. The head bounced over the thickets, rolled down the hills, and climbed along the vines. It searched through every valley but it could not find a trace of its keeper. "Pu ... Pu ... Pu...." They say that this head, nearly dying of hunger, never stops moving through the underbrush, looking for some person to whom it can attach itself, and live comfortably. Have you never seen it?

Some naked men raise their eyes to the tops of the trees, one of them speaks and the others are silent. He points out a star that flickers in the foliage, a *satellite*. There is a long silence. The stars are actually mysterious birds....

(Guayaramerin, 1966—Pucallpa, 1969)

ABOUT THE
AUTHORS

J A C Q U E S   M E U N I E R, a contributor of more than twenty years to *Le Monde,* is a poet, a traveler, and an ethnologist, as well as the author of several books, most recently *Le Monacle de Joseph Conrad* (Paris: Le Décou-verte/Le Monde, 1987).

A N N E - M A R I E   S A V A R I N is Director d'Études at the École des Haute Études en Sciences Sociales, Paris.

C A R O L   C H R I S T E N S E N ' S recent translations (with Thomas Christensen) include *Like Water for Chocolate* by Laura Esquivel and *The Harp and the Shadow* by Alejo Carpentier (Mercury House).

COVER DESIGNER: Sharon Smith
TEXT DESIGNER AND EDITOR: Thomas Christensen
TEXT TYPE: Monotype Columbus
COMPOSITION: Philip Bronson
PRODUCTION COORDINATORS:
David Peattie and Cynthia Gitter
PRINTER/BINDER: Haddon Craftsmen